12/98

P9-EEO-823

VOICES
FROM THE
CAMPS

VOICES FROM THE CAMPS

INTERNMENT OF JAPANESE AMERICANS DURING WORLD WAR II

BY LARRY DANE BRIMNER

FRANKLIN WATTS
New York – Chicago – London – Toronto – Sydney

For Those Who Remembered,
So That Others Won't Forget

Photographs copyright: ©: UPI/Bettmann: pp. 1, 2 bottom; The Library of
Congress: pp. 2 top, 7, 8, 9, 11, 12, 13, 14, 16 top, 17, 18, 22, 23, 27, 32;
Wide World Photos: pp. 3, 4, 5, 28, 29 bottom, 30, 31; The National Ar-
chives: pp. 6, 10, 15, 16 bottom, 20, 21, 24, 25, 26, 29 top; The Miyatake
Collection: p. 19.

Larry Brimner

Library of Congress Cataloging-in-Publication Data

Brimner, Larry Dane.
Voices from the camps : internment of Japanese Americans
during World War II / Larry Dane Brimner.
p.   cm.
Includes bibliographical references and index.
ISBN 0-531-11179-2
1. Japanese Americans—Evacuation and relocation, 1942–1945—
Juvenile literature. 2. World War, 1939–1945—Reparations—
Juvenile literature. [1. Japanese Americans—Evacuation and
relocation, 1942–1945. 2. World War, 1939–1945—United States.]
I. Title.
D769.8.A6B73   1994
940.53′1503956073—dc20   93-30201   CIP   AC

CONTENTS

VOICES FROM THE CAMPS

ACKNOWLEDGMENTS

Many people and institutions played a part in the development of this book. I wish to thank the following for their ideas, encouragement, and help in locating research materials: Nancy Bolger; Senator Alan Cranston and his legislative aide, Susan Vinal; Violet Kazue de-Cristoforo; Sue Kunitomi Embrey; Dr. Paul Erickson; Kris Flynn; Kim William Hunter; Victoria Mathews; Marilyn Morton; Barbara Santucci; Julie Williams; Jolene Wong; the Japanese American Citizens League (San Francisco); the Japanese American National Museum; the National Japanese American Historical Society, especially Tom Kawaguchi, Richard Tokeshi, Clifford Uyeda, and Rosalyn M. Tonai; the Japanese American Library, especially Karl Matsushita; the Eastern California Museum; the University of California at Los Angeles, Special Collections Library; the Japanese American Cultural and Community Center; the National Archives; and the Smithsonian Institution.

Special thanks to all those courageous individuals who told their moving stories before the Commission on Wartime Relocation and Internment of Civilians. The personal accounts used in this book were compiled from testimony presented at those hearings, and recorded on videotapes and audiotapes, and written transcripts. It is my fervent hope that this format does

9

justice to the poignant stories told before the commission.

Finally, I am indebted to Dr. Gordon Nakagawa, for giving me access to the videotapes and for lending his expertise in checking the manuscript for accuracy and detail; and to Dale F. Shimasaki, for his suggestions and advice.

– 1 –
"A DATE WHICH WILL LIVE IN INFAMY"

On the morning of December 7, 1941, more than three hundred Japanese planes droned above the Pacific Ocean. Their target was a United States naval base: Pearl Harbor, Hawaii.

The Japanese had calculated that they stood little chance of winning a war with the United States unless the U.S. Pacific Fleet was destroyed.[1] Vice Admiral Chuichi Nagumo, who commanded the huge Japanese strike force, launched the assault to achieve this goal, but everything depended on surprise.

As the Japanese planes advanced, people at Pearl Harbor were going about their Sunday morning routines. A skeleton crew of naval workers prepared for the day ahead, while a few early-rising beach combers strolled along the Hawaiian shore. Commander Mitsuo Fuchida, leading the air strike, saw the ships of the American fleet lined up like ducks in an amusement park arcade. Battleship row, it was called. Even before the first bomb fell, Fuchida was so sure of victory that he signaled back to Nagumo aboard the Japanese carrier *Akagi* that the surprise attack was a success.[2] Then, at about 7:49 A.M., the bombardment—and with it America's war with Japan—began.

By 8:54 A.M. the attack on Pearl Harbor was over. In the strike's wake, 19 ships were either sunk or crippled, and more than 100 planes at nearby airfields were destroyed, most while sitting on the ground. The human toll was even greater. More than 2,400 American lives were lost, almost half of those aboard the battleship *Arizona* when it blew up. Another 1,178 were wounded. Japanese losses were considerably less: 29 planes and 55 airmen.[3] While it marked a great Japanese victory, Pearl Harbor was the worst military disaster in American history. The losses were so staggering that shock waves radiated throughout the country, and anger and fear swelled.

The following day, President Franklin Delano Roosevelt went to Capitol Hill to address a joint session of Congress. The ailing President made his way into the House Chamber on the arm of his son James, a marine captain, and he was greeted with applause. Even the Republicans joined in, the attack on Pearl Harbor having united Congress and, in a greater sense, the country behind the President. With one act of hostility directed against American citizens, isolationists suddenly became interventionists. The President stood alone at the rostrum and carefully measured his words: "Yesterday, December 7, 1941—a date which will live in infamy—the United States of America was suddenly and deliberately attacked by naval and air forces of the Empire of Japan." In a speech lasting only six minutes, President Roosevelt asked Congress to declare war on the Empire of Japan. Within an hour the Senate and House of Representatives acted upon the President's request, with only one dissenting vote (by Representative Jeannette Rankin of Montana).[4] Three days later Germany and Italy countered with declarations of war against the United States—and the world was at war.

There was another casualty of Pearl Harbor, one often overlooked or mentioned only briefly in our history books. At the time of the strike on Pearl Harbor, some 127,000 persons of Japanese ancestry were living in the United States, most of them residing in the three Pacific Coast states—Washington, Oregon, and California. Of these, nearly 80 percent lived in California, where anti-Asian prejudice historically ran deep.[5] The Japanese were linked in people's minds with the Chinese, who had preceded them to the United States to build the railroads, and Caucasians saw the ethnic Japanese as economic competitors, just as they had the Chinese. Two out of every three Japanese were American citizens by birth and one-third were forbidden by law to become citizens because anti-Asian groups had successfully lobbied lawmakers to enforce America's original naturalization law, which limited citizenship to "free white persons." For these residents, the attack on Pearl Harbor unleashed a dark period in American history. It was a period when civil liberties were suspended without any formal accusations or charges being made and when the guarantees under the Bill of Rights were ignored.[6] It was a time often described by today's scholars and legal experts as the most brazen example of racism and the most blatant breach of individual rights in the history of the United States.[7]

Public outcry and political pressure called for something to be done about the "Japanese problem" within the United States. Specifically, the cry was for total removal of anybody of Japanese ancestry, citizen or not. So strong was the sentiment that it carried over to the floor of the House of Representatives, where Congressman Rankin declared, "I'm for catching every Japanese in America, Alaska, and Hawaii now and putting them in concentration camps ... Damn them! Let's get rid of them now!"[8] Pearl Harbor triggered a war on two fronts: one against an enemy in the Pacific, the other against an imagined enemy within our own borders. In spite of Amendment IV to the Constitution, a guarantee "against unreasonable searches and seizures," the homes of legal American residents were entered and searched. Amendment V's guarantee that no person shall "be deprived of life, liberty, or property, without due process of law" did nothing to protect old men—community leaders—who were rounded up and jailed, or their families, who were ordered out of their homes and, later, their communities. With total disregard for the Bill of Rights, 110,000 persons of Japanese ancestry—two-thirds of them citizens and most not old enough to vote—were uprooted and forced to evacuate to what the government antiseptically termed "relocation" centers. Their only "crime" was that of looking Japanese. The number of internees swelled eventually to 120,000.[9]

Woven into the pages that follow are the voices of these victims of Pearl Harbor, voices that have long been silent. It's true that their testimony lacks the historian's broad view of World War II. But it is often the personal detail that makes history believable and unforgettable and causes one to realize the human toll that war exacts.

Paul Chikahisa described December 7, 1941: "The day after my twelfth birthday my younger brother and I were in a theater when suddenly there was an announcement which brought apprehension, fear, and uncertainty to me. It was announced that all military personnel were to report to their base. I don't recall if we left then or at the end of the movie, but it seemed as though all the eyes were watching us."

Paul's perception wasn't without reason. Many Issei, members of the immigrant generation from Japan, and the American-born Nisei, were confused by the distrust and enmity of Caucasian Americans. One Nisei, a seventh-grader at the time, recalled that when "the war started ... my brother was in sixth grade.... One day he came home from school and told me that the teacher

14

did not let him and two other Nisei students stand to sing 'The Star-Spangled Banner.' "

To be of Japanese ancestry in the days, weeks, and months following Pearl Harbor was to be regarded as the enemy. For most of the American public, fear of the "yellow peril" had been reawakened.

– 2 –
"NOT BONA FIDE CITIZENS"

Anti-Asian prejudice had a long history on the West Coast of the United States, beginning with the influx of Chinese in the middle of the nineteenth century. Chinese immigrants provided much of the cheap labor needed to complete the transcontinental railroad. When east and west were connected by rail, the laborers were let go and almost ten thousand unemployed Chinese were dumped into the job market. Unfortunately, jobs were scarce and the economy of the 1870s was weak. Chinese laborers, though, were willing to work for lower wages than were most Caucasians.[1]

As a result, feelings of hostility erupted. Protests were directed against the Chinese and their employers. Labor movements, especially those in California, used anti-Chinese sentiment as an organizing tool. Their first claims were that the Chinese presented unfair labor competition. Later, cries of racial inferiority and injury to Western civilization were leveled against the immigrants. It wasn't long before the press began to aggravate the situation by taking an anti-Chinese stance. Headlines alerted readers to the so-called yellow peril, stirring both fear and hatred. Articles claimed that a high Chinese birthrate would eventually result in swarms of Chinese overpowering the Caucasian population and subjugating them to slavery.[2] The Democratic and Republican parties sensed the mood of the electorate. Both parties jumped on the bandwagon by adopting anti-Chinese planks in their platforms.

Pressures mounted for the federal government to do something. Under that pressure, President Chester Arthur signed into law the Chinese Exclusion Act of 1882, a ten-year ban on Chinese immigration. It was renewed in 1892 and made permanent in 1902.[3]

The Japanese began to trickle into the United States soon after Commodore Matthew Perry's expedition to Japan in 1853. Jobs were scarce in Japan in the last half of the nineteenth century; rapid industrialization had displaced many laborers.[4] But across the Pacific, America offered promise of a brighter future, as it had to a tide of European immigrants.

The United States, rebounding from the recession of the 1870s and drained of manpower by the Alaska gold rush of the late 1890s, began to look for a new source of cheap labor. The Chinese Exclusion Act of 1892 effectively ruled out a new influx of Chinese laborers, so both industry and agriculture recruited the Japanese.[5] These new settlers sent reports back to their homeland about better economic conditions in the United States and vast vistas of unpopulated land, and more and more Japanese immigrants were drawn to this country.

Like many other immigrants, the first Japanese to come to the United States were mostly young adult males, who were both eager and ambitious.[6] They brought with them farming and fishing skills, and they were strong and willing to work for little money. They supplied the labor necessary to complete work on the railroad connecting Seattle with the East. The Japanese immigrants cultivated marginal lands and turned them into productive farms. They revolutionized the fishing industry.

But the Japanese remained insular. Besides manual

skills, they brought their customs, traditions, and religion, which set them apart from the mainstream. Since they were already excluded from political life by laws barring them from becoming citizens, they were segregated, and they socialized among their own, often speaking their native language. These factors, combined with the long-standing hostility to the Chinese, isolated them from general society and made them an easy target of racism. On May 7, 1900, San Francisco Mayor James Phelan expressed the popular sentiment: "The Japanese are starting the same tide of immigration which we thought we had checked twenty years ago. . . . The Chinese and Japanese are not bona fide citizens. They are not the stuff of which American citizens can be made."[7]

In the same year the American Federation of Labor asked Congress to extend the Chinese exclusion law to all "Mongolian" labor. Members cited unfair labor competition; they charged the Chinese and Japanese with stealing jobs from hardworking, loyal Americans. Both the Democratic and Republican parties again succumbed to public pressure and adopted anti-Japanese planks in their platforms. Politicians enthusiastically embraced the issue in order to win votes and whip up racist attitudes, which resulted in an even greater number of anti-Asian activities. By 1905, the Japanese Exclusion League, made up largely of labor groups, had formed to enact legislation that would end Japanese immigration, bar land ownership by Japanese, and segregate schoolchildren of Japanese ancestry.[8] Some school districts, including many in the San Francisco Bay area, bowed to the pressure and barred Asian children from white primary schools.

Although the United States had a history of racism and segregation—blacks in the South were unable to attend white schools—such actions strained relations

18

with Japan. President Theodore Roosevelt, embarrassed by the actions and wishing to maintain sound diplomatic relations with Japan, negotiated with California to rescind segregation orders and to refrain from passing further anti-Japanese legislation. He complained to California's governor that "in the event of war it will be the Nation as a whole that will pay the consequences."[9] In return, he promised to negotiate with Japan to restrict immigration. What resulted was known as the "Gentlemen's Agreement," under which Japan agreed to restrict passports, except to "laborers who have already been in America and to the parents, wives, and children of laborers already resident there."[10]

The Gentlemen's Agreement of 1907 slowed the pace of immigration but did not end it. However, that didn't stop politicians from touting the agreement as the solution to what the *San Francisco Chronicle* had called "The Japanese Invasion, the Problem of the Hour."[11]

Many Issei men continued to arrange marriages and bring their brides to this country. At the time, arranged marriages were traditional in Japan, as in many other parts of the world. The new brides would set sail for America and would meet their husbands for the first time at the dock in California. Called picture brides, because they were usually identified by pictures sent ahead to the men, their arrival created the illusion that Japan had violated the Gentlemen's Agreement.

To stem the continuing emigration from Japan and spurred on by farmers who feared competition, the California state legislature passed the Alien Land Law of 1913, which barred land purchases by aliens who were ineligible for citizenship.[12] By this time, however, many Issei had children who had been born in the United States. The children were legal citizens under the Con-

19

stitution and provided a way for the Issei to get around the restrictive law. Many Issei purchased property in their children's names and acted as guardians.

New calls were heard for a total ban on emigration from Japan. Four major organizations led the protest: the Native Sons and Native Daughters of the Golden West, the American Legion, the California State Federation of Labor, and the California State Grange Association.[13] They joined forces with other anti-Japanese groups, most notably the California Joint Immigration Committee—formerly called the Japanese Exclusion League. As a result, a five-point plan was adopted by the legislature in which the Gentlemen's Agreement would be canceled, picture brides would be denied entry, further emigration from Japan would be prohibited, Asians would be forever barred from American citizenship, and no child born in the United States would be granted citizenship unless both parents were of a race eligible for citizenship.[14] Similar racist legislation was sought in Arizona, Washington, and Oregon.

Largely because the Gentlemen's Agreement had been presented as an exclusion act, most people wrongly believed that Japan wasn't living up to the terms of the agreement. V. S. McClatchy, the wealthy retired publisher of the *Sacramento Bee*, and California Senator Hiram Johnson led the fight in the 1920s for a total ban on Japanese immigration.[15] In 1924 their efforts paid off and the federal immigration law was changed to expressly exclude the Japanese.

To many Americans, Japan's alignment with Nazi Germany and Fascist Italy in 1940 only confirmed the threat of the yellow peril. The attack on Pearl Harbor fixed in the national mind the image of hordes of "yellow-skinned barbarians" invading America's shores to overpower the Caucasian population. Also suspect was the loyalty of all persons of Japanese ancestry living in the United States. Might they represent a fifth column—

20

a secret subversive group of residents in league with the enemy? Suspicion of the Issei and Nisei seemed not only acceptable but patriotic as well.

Even simple fishermen were suspect. Charles Hamasaki was just eighteen when FBI agents burst into his Terminal Island house in the middle of the night. "[They arrested me] just because I was a fisherman and I knew the coastline, how deep the water was, and this and that." Forty years after the attack on Pearl Harbor, Charlie was able to scoff at their suspicions. "You think I knew all that stuff? I didn't know nothing.... Some people ... say fishing boat carry torpedo. Where the hell they [the fishermen] going to get torpedo?"

In the weeks following the disaster at Pearl Harbor, Charlie's world was drastically altered by brazen racism. Calls to round up and relocate persons of Japanese ancestry had been heard. All that remained to set the wheels in motion was the endorsement by the president of the United States of America.

– 3 –
"IT JUST COULDN'T HAPPEN IN A DEMOCRACY"

On February 19, 1942, ten weeks after the attack on Pearl Harbor, Franklin Delano Roosevelt signed Executive Order 9066. To protect "against espionage and against sabotage to national-defense material, national-defense premises and national-defense utilities," the president directed "the Secretary of War, and the Military Commanders whom he may from time to time designate ... to prescribe military areas ... from which any or all persons may be excluded."[1]

Although there was no direct mention of resident Japanese aliens or their American-born offspring, the executive order was obviously aimed squarely at all residents of Japanese descent. Much later, when there was talk of using the order to move Germans and Italians on the East Coast, the president wrote that he considered enemy alien control to be a civilian matter except "in the case of the Japanese ... on the Pacific Coast."[2] Clearly the president had endorsed racism and Japanese exclusion, even though many of those Japanese happened also to be American citizens.

Was exclusion vital to national security? Germany had used resident agents and sympathizers—the so-called fifth column—to get a foothold in other countries. It was anticipated that Japan might employ the same tactic. Extensive surveillance, however, suggested otherwise.

The Japanese living on the West Coast were investigated by the Federal Bureau of Investigation, the Navy Department, and President Roosevelt's own network of informants. J. Edgar Hoover, director of the FBI, concluded that calls for a mass exclusion of the Japanese were a result of political pressures and had no basis in reality.[3] Prior to the attack on Pearl Harbor, the FBI already had a list of potentially dangerous individuals and saw no serious threat to the security of the United States from the majority of resident alien Japanese or from the Nisei.[4] Indeed, the FBI had concluded that in Japan there was widespread distrust of the Issei; they had, after all, turned their back on their native land. The Nisei, for all practical purposes, were regarded as foreigners by Japan. The FBI reported that sabotage, if it did happen, would most likely be committed by individuals already identified by the authorities or by Caucasian agents hired by Japan. Caucasian agents would be far less conspicuous and more able to move freely in sensitive areas than would any person of Japanese ancestry.

Lieutenant Commander K. D. Ringle of the Office of Naval Intelligence stated in the Report of the Commission on Wartime Relocation and Internment of Civilians that the large majority of ethnic Japanese were at least passively loyal to the United States. According to *Personal Justice Denied*, "Ringle saw no need for mass action against people of Japanese ancestry."[5]

Perhaps the most significant of all the intelligence reports was the so-called Munson Report. The President periodically relied on John Franklin Carter, a journalist, to obtain information from outside the government. At Carter's request, Curtis B. Munson, a well-to-do Chicago businessman, began looking into the loyalty of the Issei

23

and Nisei. On November 7, 1941, Carter forwarded Munson's report to the President. Munson wrote:

> *There is no Japanese "problem" on the Coast. There will be no armed uprising of Japanese. There will undoubtedly be some sabotage financed by Japan and executed largely by imported agents or agents already imported. There will be the odd case of fanatical sabotage by some Japanese "crackpot." In each Naval District there are about 250 to 300 suspects under surveillance. It is easy to get on the suspect list, merely a speech in favor of Japan at some banquet being sufficient to land one there. The Intelligence Services are generous with the title of suspect and are taking no chances. Privately, they believe that only 50 or 60 in each district can be classed as really dangerous. The Japanese are hampered as saboteurs because of their easily recognized physical appearance. It will be hard for them to get near anything to blow up if it is guarded. [emphasis added] ... The Japanese here is almost exclusively a farmer, a fisherman, or a small businessman.[6]*

Yet in spite of overwhelming evidence to the contrary, reports of fifth column activity abounded. After an inspection of Pearl Harbor following the bombing, Secretary of the Navy Frank Knox returned to the mainland to tell the press that the disastrous losses in Hawaii were the result of the work of a fifth column. There was no evidence to back up his claim. In fact, General Walter C. Short, who had been in command at the time of the attack, refuted the claim. Nevertheless, West Coast newspapers gave major attention to the Secretary's story and reinforced the mounting race-based fear.[7]

Ringle and Munson believed there was no more to fear from the resident Japanese than from any other ethnic group living in the United States. Hoover recommended surveillance, not detention and exclusion. But these views were not heard over more vocal calls that something be done about the "enemy alien problem." Henry McLemore, a syndicated columnist for the *San Francisco Examiner*, wrote on January 29, 1942: "I am for immediate removal of every Japanese on the West Coast to a point deep in the interior. I don't mean a nice part of the interior either. Herd 'em up, pack 'em off and give 'em the inside room in the badlands. Let 'em be pinched, hurt, hungry and dead up against it. . . . Let us have no patience with the enemy or with anyone whose veins carry his blood.

"Personally, I hate the Japanese. And that goes for all of them."[8]

Tensions were running high. The Nisei tried to divert the gathering storm clouds by displaying American flags in their windows. They planted victory gardens to help with the war effort. They purchased war bonds. One group in Fresno, California, even wired Congress offering their services in the struggle against Japan.[9] But their efforts did little to check suspicion or to stem the rising tide of prejudice.

The army in particular was concerned that Japanese residents were sending radio transmissions to Japanese ships offshore. Cameras, weapons, radio transmitters, and any other equipment that might be used in espionage and sabotage had been confiscated by police and FBI agents immediately following the attack on Pearl Harbor. But this didn't allay people's fears. Henry Yamaga recalled that "a police patrol came to my house to ask me whether I had a short wave radio. I told them that I had a set, but the short wave had been disconnected by the radio repairman and that I had a certificate to show that I had [conformed] to the government order. But they told me that when they went by my house, they experienced static in their radio. They were sure a message was being sent to an enemy submarine off the Pacific coast.... I asked the police to check every house on my street.... I rode with them in a patrol car cruising slowly to each house. Soon the interference became louder and louder, and we finally stopped at the home of a house painter ... a Caucasian. He would come home from work ... and take a shower and shave. When he started to shave, the electric current caused the static in the police radio to sound like a coded message."

Jack Fujimoto, who was thirteen at the outbreak of the war and living on his family's truck farm in southern California, remembered similar encounters with officials. "We packed much produce late at night for early morning shipment," he said. "On at least two occasions, FBI agents appeared to inspect our home and inquire about 'Where's your signal equipment? Why do you signal boats offshore?' "

No one of Japanese ancestry escaped scrutiny. Suspicions ran wild and would have been comical had it not been for the seriousness of their nature. One man, a Buddhist priest in Salinas, California, at the time of the attack on Pearl Harbor, recalled that local police told him he had to take his church bell down. The police were afraid that "the church bell might be used to signal the Japanese naval force to attack the Monterey Naval facilities which was [sic] good nineteen miles away. With a good wind blowing, perhaps we would have been lucky to ... [send a signal] a little bit, but not that far, certainly."

Two months later, in February 1942, FBI agents from San Francisco took the priest and two others into custody and photographed them. That same day, the San Francisco Chronicle carried the photograph with a caption reporting that "three Japanese priests were apprehended for their activities." The suggestion of sabotage was clear, even without specific reference to it. It wasn't long before Life magazine ballyhooed the roundup of

26

these and other Buddhist priests as positive proof of fifth column activity, and pointed to church public address systems and multicolored flags as instruments of sabotage. The priest explained that the public address systems were just that—public address systems—and "the flags . . . were used . . . by the Sunday school youngsters as a part of their . . . normal learning activities."

The apprehension of Buddhist priests and other community leaders was swift following the attack on Pearl Harbor. Mitsuo Usui tells this story: "I was attending Saint Mary's Episcopal Church on the Sunday morning that the war broke out. . . . When I reached home later that day, I found my mother in hysterics, crying and trying to pick up after the FBI had searched the house. 'They took Papa!' Mama shouted. 'They chained him and numbered him like an animal.' We called the police station to find out where they had taken him, but it was of no avail."

In most cases, those immediately taken into custody were old men. Leaving behind their wives and children when they were taken away by the FBI, they usually were not able to tell their families where they were going or when they would return. In some cases, entire families were torn apart. Sixteen-year-old Peter Ota was one who witnessed the devastation of the family he had known.

December 7, 1941, was a traumatic day for my mother, father and sister, and me. The events from that day were to eventually separate my family, my father's business was to be wiped out overnight, and my mother was to spend her final days a thousand miles away from her family. During the evening of December 7 . . . my father, who was part of a wedding party, was literally pulled out of the wedding wearing a full dress tuxedo. . . .

For several days there was absolutely no infor-

mation as to his well-being. . . . Days passed, and we had no idea what had happened to him. Inquiries produced no new information, and we were becoming frantic with no knowledge of his whereabouts. We finally received word that he was sent to Fort Missoula, Montana. . . . In one fateful day, our nation labeled him an enemy alien, a threat to our national security. . . .

My mother became very despondent over the imprisonment of my father, and she became seriously ill shortly after December 7. She had contracted tuberculosis, and she was finally sent to the Olive View Sanitarium in La Crescenta, California. In April of 1942, when Executive Order 9066 forced us to evacuate from the West Coast, my [thirteen-year-old] sister . . . and I . . . packed only what we could carry and we proceeded to the Santa Anita Assembly Center. The injustices resulting from the war hysteria finally devastated our family, and my sister and I were completely separated from our parents.

Egged on by the press and a fearful army, rumors of signals being sent to Japanese ships offshore persisted. Lieutenant General John L. DeWitt, in charge of the army's Western Defense Command (comprising Washington, Oregon, California, and Arizona), did little to calm fears and suspicions. DeWitt had seen how quickly General Short was forced out of the military after the disaster at Pearl Harbor. He had no intention of letting his guard down and suffering the same fate. While the Justice Department and the War Department fought over the constitutionality of exclusion, DeWitt pressed for the immediate withdrawal of persons of Japanese ancestry from the Western Defense Command. His position was bolstered—and, some suggest, engineered—by the War Department's Major General Allen W. Gullion and Major Karl R. Bendetsen.[10] In spite of reports from

28

the Federal Communications Commission, which monitored radio broadcasts, that illegal transmissions were minimal, and despite the FBI's concurrence with the FCC reports, DeWitt accepted every rumor as fact. Major General Joseph W. Stilwell, who served with DeWitt, summed it up this way in his diary: "Common sense is thrown to the winds and any absurdity is believed."[11]

Most Nisei believed that any roundup and exclusion would involve only the Issei. After all, the Nisei, born on American soil, were legal American citizens. They were troubled by the open racism, to be sure, but they believed that the Constitution of the United States of America would protect them. "When I read and heard rumors that all Japanese would be interned, I couldn't believe it," said Mabel Ota. "I kept saying that I was a loyal American citizen and that it just couldn't happen in a democracy."

DeWitt, charged with making sure that no repetition of Pearl Harbor occurred on the West Coast, wasn't willing to take any chances. He urged random raids on the homes of ethnic Japanese but encountered opposition from U.S. Attorney General Francis Biddle, who argued that constitutional guarantees prohibited this unless there was probable cause. DeWitt countered that ancestry *was* probable cause.[12]

In January, DeWitt recommended to Henry L. Stimson, the secretary of war, the establishment in the coastal states of 135 "prohibited zones" and a number of larger "restricted zones." To James Rowe, the assistant attorney general, he spoke of the Japanese: "I have no confidence in their loyalty whatsoever."[13]

A short time later, DeWitt clarified his position to Stimson:

> *The area lying to the west of Cascade and Sierra Nevada Mountains in Washington, Oregon and California, is highly critical not only because the lines of*

communication and supply to the Pacific theater pass
through it, but also because of the vital industrial
production therein, particularly aircraft. In the war
in which we are now engaged racial affinities are not
severed by migration. The Japanese race is an enemy
race and while many second and third generation
Japanese born on United States soil, possessed of
United States citizenship, have become "American-
ized," the racial strains are undiluted. To conclude
otherwise is to expect that children born of white
parents on Japanese soil sever all racial affinity and
become loyal Japanese subjects, ready to fight and,
if necessary, to die for Japan in a war against the
nation of their parents. . . . It, therefore, follows that
along the vital Pacific Coast over 112,000 potential
enemies, of Japanese extraction, are at large today.
There are indications that these are organized and
ready for concerted action at a favorable opportu-
nity. The very fact that no sabotage has taken place
to date is a disturbing and confirming indication that
such action will be taken.[14]

DeWitt's justification for wanting to remove the ethnic
Japanese from the West Coast was that there had been
no acts of sabotage. Such lack of action, in DeWitt's
eyes, was proof that there eventually would be. This
notion not only defies any and all logic, but it also allows
the racism beneath his words to seep to the surface.

By this time, the cry to evacuate the ethnic Japanese
from the West Coast was being echoed in all quarters.
On January 29, the *San Francisco Examiner* ran the
following headline: "Removal of All S.F. Japs Urged;
State Bans Jobs to Aliens." Another headline, also in the
San Francisco Examiner of January 29, warned: "Disaster on West Coast Predicted." The ensuing article
quoted Representative Martin Dies of Texas, who had
delivered a passionate plea before Congress, saying that

"unless this Government adopts an alert attitude toward this whole question, there will occur on the west coast a tragedy which will make Pearl Harbor sink into insignificance compared with it. . . . No nation can defeat the uniformed soldiers of the enemy unless it first defeats the un-uniformed soldiers of the enemy in its midst." Clearly, politicians had found a popular cause.

Congressman Clarence Lea, on behalf of the congressional delegation from California, Oregon, and Washington, wrote to President Roosevelt:

> We recommend the immediate evacuation of all persons of Japanese lineage and all others, aliens and citizens alike, whose presence shall be deemed dangerous or inimical to the defense of the United States from all strategic areas. . . .
>
> We make these recommendations in order that no citizen, located in a strategic area, may cloak his disloyalty or subversive activity under the mantle of his citizenship alone and further to guarantee protection to all loyal persons, alien and citizen alike, whose safety may be endangered by some wanton act of sabotage.[15]

Others who demanded exclusion were more forthright. Their motives didn't include concern about national security and weren't masked by the pretense of providing protection for loyal citizens of Japanese ancestry. In "The People Nobody Wants," an article appearing in the *Saturday Evening Post* on May 9, 1942, author Frank J. Taylor quoted Austin Anson, of the Vegetable Grower-Shipper Association: "We're charged with wanting to get rid of the Japs for selfish reasons. We might as well be honest. We do. It's a question of whether the white man lives on the Pacific Coast or the brown man."[16]

Oddly, calls to relocate the ethnic Japanese living in Hawaii were only minor compared to the clamor along the West Coast. Though thousands of miles closer to the enemy and strategic to America's defense, Hawaii needed every available laborer. As a result, the ethnic Japanese in Hawaii, while they were looked on with suspicion, fared better than those on the mainland and had their constitutional rights upheld to a far greater degree.

Still, it was in this climate of hostility, racism, paranoia, and greed, that Franklin Delano Roosevelt issued Executive Order 9066. Terminal Island, Los Angeles, California, was placed under the jurisdiction of the navy, and on February 25 the residents were given forty-eight hours to leave the island. In rapid succession, General DeWitt created military zones and directed all persons of Japanese ancestry, regardless of citizenship status, to evacuate Bainbridge Island, Washington. A curfew required that all enemy aliens and ethnic Japanese be in their homes between 8:00 P.M. and 6:00 A.M.

The course of American history had been set by Executive Order 9066. In spite of the fact that no Japanese American was *ever* charged with, brought to trial for, or convicted of any act of espionage or sabotage, the way was cleared for individuals and groups to be excluded from specific areas based, at least officially, on military necessity. Joe Kimoto recalled asking himself, "Why did this thing happen to me now?"

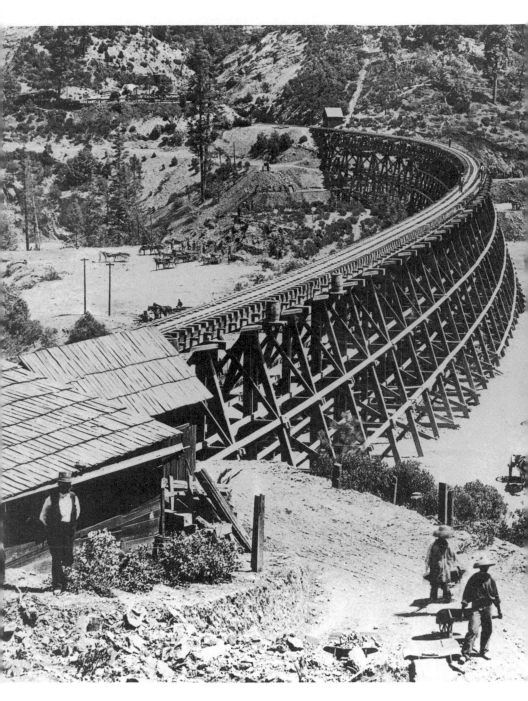

Among the first Asian immigrants to the United States were the Chinese workers who were brought to this country to build the transcontinental railroad.

Japanese farmers in California in the early 1900s. Many ethnic Japanese continued to be farmers until World War II.

Below: Japanese "picture brides" on their arrival in California in 1920 to join their new husbands. A congressional committee (right) examines their passports.

*The Japanese aerial attack on Pearl Harbor was a
preemptive strike against the United States Navy's
Pacific Fleet. The battleships* USS West Virginia, USS
Tennessee, *and USS* Arizona *were casualties of the
Japanese bombs.*

*President Franklin D. Roosevelt moments after
asking Congress for a declaration of war
against Japan*

An FBI agent searches the home of a Japanese-American family immediately after the attack on Pearl Harbor.

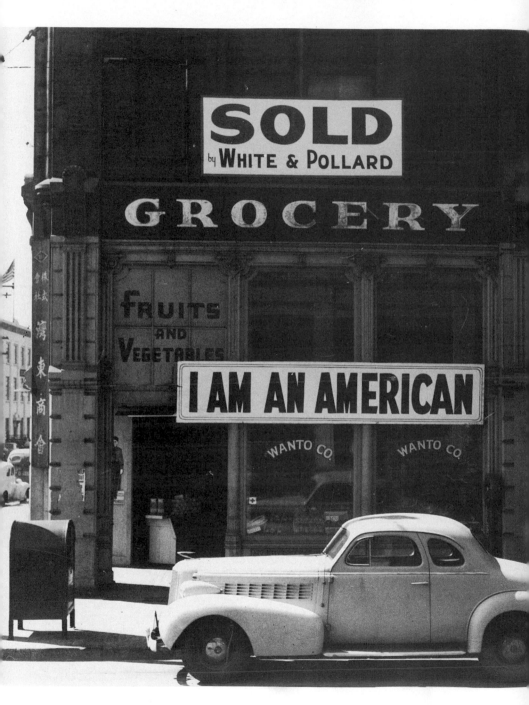

*Nisei merchants displayed signs proclaiming their
citizenship to allay the fears and suspicions of
their fellow citizens.*

Once the United States was at war with Japan, Japanese-Americans tried to show their loyalty to the United States.

*Notices were posted instructing citizens of
Japanese ancestry to register for relocation.*

*Japanese-Americans stand in line to receive numbers
for their families and instructions to follow
for their relocation.*

*Japanese-Americans were forced to sell everything
they had, including their businesses, in order to
comply with the evacuation orders. This fishing boat
had to be put up for sale.*

*This plant nursery owned by a Japanese-American
had to be sold.*

As the evacuation progressed, Japanese-American evacuees were forced to sell their property at cut-rate prices. As a result, they lost everything they had worked for all their lives.

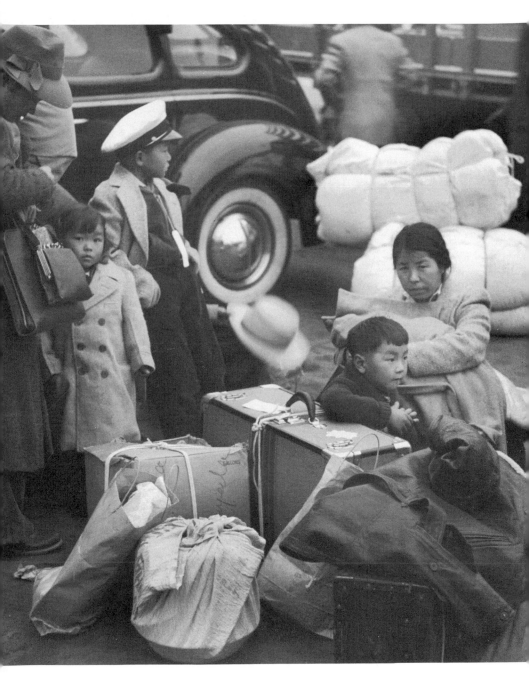

*Families sit with their belongings as they await
transportation to the assembly center. Note the tags
on the children and the suitcases.*

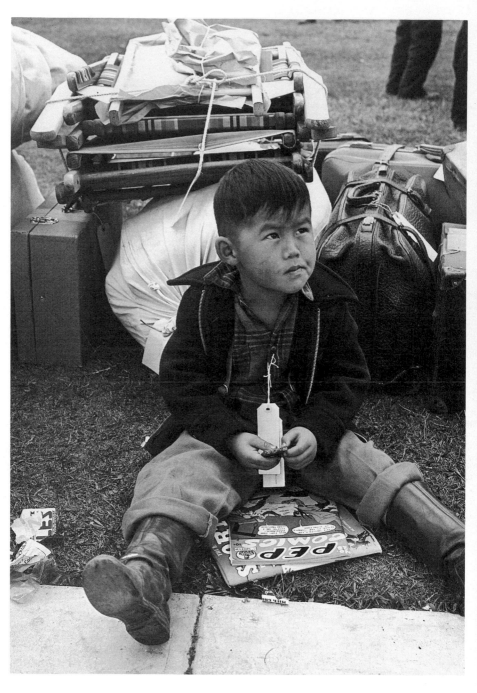

This child has been given a number and a tag
for the journey to an assembly center.

These evacuees are being sent to an assembly center and from there to an internment camp. Even so, this little boy demonstrates his loyalty to the United States.

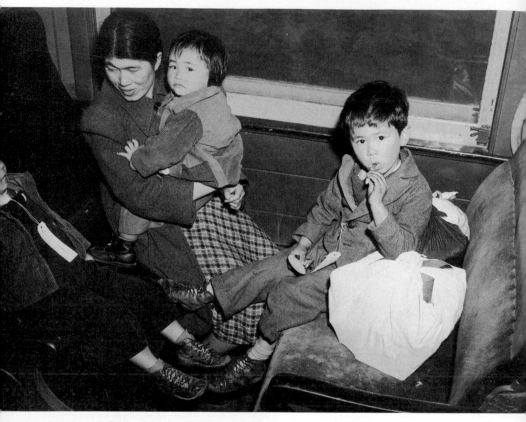

This mother and children are traveling by train to an internment camp. The little boys wear the relocation tags.

On the train to the internment camp

– 4 –
"DEMOCRACY CAN BE AN ILLUSION"

"We all wore tags with numbers," remembered Amy Iwasaki Mass, who was six years old when she and her family boarded a bus for the Pomona Assembly Center. "Each family lined up with the oldest member of the family at the head of the line, the youngest at the end. I was scared. I was the youngest and I wanted to be closer to my parents."

Mandatory evacuation had begun. It started with the posting of notices announcing that the head of each household was required to register all family members at a post office. It ended in lines of people waiting to board buses and trains that would take them to assembly centers. Emily Medvec describes it this way in her introduction to Ansel Adams's *Born Free and Equal*: "By the spring of 1942, they were suddenly a people without any constitutional freedom—whose faces were an exact likeness of the enemy."[1]

Prior to this, there had been attempts to have the ethnic Japanese relocate "voluntarily." As directed by Secretary of War Henry L. Stimson, General DeWitt created Military Area No. 1 along the western half of Washington, Oregon, and California and in the southern half of Arizona. Everything else west of the Mississippi fell into Military Area No. 2. These boundaries were established on March 2 by DeWitt's Military Public Proclamation No. 1. The proclamation also designated a number of prohibited zones to which the military controlled access and, of course, from which the ethnic Japanese were excluded. While the Issei and Nisei were told to leave the prohibited areas, they were only "encouraged" to settle outside of Military Area No. 1, as DeWitt warned that all of Military Area No. 1 might eventually be redesignated a prohibited zone.[2]

Many complied with DeWitt's Proclamation by selling out and moving inland to Military Zone No. 2. Most did not. Liquidating property and businesses and uprooting families wasn't easily accomplished on short notice. Compounding the difficulty, many of the community's men had been rounded up by the FBI shortly after the attack on Pearl Harbor. Women and children unaccustomed to handling financial transactions were ill equipped to settle affairs. "Voluntary" evacuation came at a bad time for farmers, too. Harvest was not far off, and most would face financial ruin if the crops were left untended.

In addition to these economic considerations, the ethnic Japanese were unsure of the reception they'd receive in new areas. Most local residents believed that the inland areas were just as vulnerable to sabotage as Military Area No. 1. Dams and railroads and bridges and electrical generating plants could be attacked so as to create widespread havoc. If the Japanese couldn't be trusted inside Military Area No. 1, they reasoned, then neither could they be trusted outside of it. Governor E. P. Carville of Nevada wrote to General DeWitt to express his views: "I do not desire that Nevada be made a dumping ground for enemy aliens to be going anywhere they might see fit to travel."[3] Governor Clark, of Idaho, had more colorful views: "Japs live like rats, breed like rats, and act like rats. We don't want them buying or leasing land and becoming permanently located in our state."[4]

34

Racism made a vivid impact on many ethnic Japanese. During her family's forced evacuation, young Amy Iwasaki Mass was struck by "the hatred in the eyes of the man and the woman who ran a restaurant in Butte, Montana." Up against such open anti-Japanese sentiment, the majority of ethnic Japanese weren't eager to rush into an unknown and unfamiliar landscape. So it was that most remained in their homes and businesses and on their farms. Within Roosevelt's own administration, opponents of the voluntary relocation program argued it was unlikely that guilty parties would voluntarily abandon their targets at the request of the government. They warned DeWitt that a voluntary plan was *voluntary* senseless and sure to fail. And so voluntary evacuation *evacuation* was scrapped.

The army acknowledged the failure on March 27, when General DeWitt released Military Public Proclamation No. 4, which prohibited all persons of Japanese ancestry from moving out of Military Area No. 1 without military approval. Henceforth the army itself would supervise the relocation and place the ethnic Japanese in what it called "pioneer" communities.

But time was of the essence. Japan was winning victory after victory in the Pacific, and America's West Coast had to be secured. Moving persons of Japanese ancestry away from the coast would not only secure the coastline from internal sabotage but would also help boost civilian morale, which was waning in the wake of the Pacific defeats. Moreover, exclusion was a popular maneuver that could promote many West Coast political and military careers. And some scholars now agree that at least some thought was given to holding a large population of "hostages," whose fate lay in the hands of the American military, as an additional bargaining tool to use with the emperor of Japan should such negotiations become necessary.[5]

The "evacuation," as it came to be called, would be

a two-step process. While sites for permanent pioneer communities were being found and housing built, temporary accommodations would be provided for the evacuees. The Wartime Civil Control Administration was formed, with newly promoted Colonel Karl R. Bendetsen in charge, to oversee the evacuation and operate the temporary sites.[6] These came to be called "assembly centers," though they were in reality fairgrounds and racetracks that had been swiftly converted to house people instead of animals.

So that not too many military troops would be occupied with the evacuation and day-to-day operation of the more permanent sites, the relocation centers were placed under direction of a newly formed agency, the War Relocation Authority (WRA). It was headed by Milton S. Eisenhower, brother of General Dwight D. Eisenhower, a future president of the United States.[7]

The first civilian exclusion orders appeared on March 31, 1942.[8] The heads of Japanese families, both alien and non-alien, were to report to control stations to receive instructions for relocating. Each family was assigned a number and told that family members could take with them only what they could carry. In some cases, evacuees had only forty-eight hours' notice to liquidate their property and possessions. Others had as much as two weeks.

Stan Yamashita, whose father had been arrested by the FBI, had bitter memories of the pervasive bewilderment when exclusion notices were posted on Terminal Island and residents were given just forty-eight hours to vacate. He asked, "Without the head of the family, how does a mother with three children move out of a house where they have lived for years?" Fear also gripped the communities. People began to destroy anything that might link them to Japan and its emperor. Bill Nakagawa remembered his mother telling him to

36

destroy all "her Japanese records that she loved so dearly. I asked her, 'Why couldn't we keep them stored somewhere?' and she replied that she didn't want to keep something that may get us into trouble later on."

Beyond confusion and fear, the exclusion notices brought with them a horde of scavengers. Yoshihiko Fujikawa, another Terminal Islander, described this scene: "It was during these forty-eight hours that I witnessed unscrupulous vultures in the form of human beings taking advantage of bewildered housewives whose husbands had been rounded up by the FBI within forty-eight hours after Pearl Harbor. They were offered pittances for practically new furniture and appliances: refrigerators, radio consoles, etc., as well as cars, and many were falling prey to these people."

Hiroshi Kamei recalled, "Our house was in from Garden Grove Boulevard about 200 yards on a dirt driveway, and on the day before the posted evacuation date, there was a lineup of cars in our driveway extending about another 200 yards in both directions along Garden Grove Boulevard, waiting their turn to come to our house." It seemed that former friends, _greed_ neighbors, and business associates turned into opportunists overnight. Roy Abbey testified that "[p]eople who were like vultures swooped down on us going through our belongings offering us a fraction of their value. When we complained to them of the low price they would respond by saying, '[Y]ou can't take it with you so take it or leave it.' "

With forced liquidation on such short notice, losses were significant and evacuees had little choice except to take what was offered for their property and possessions. Hiroshi Kamei told this story: "One man wanted to buy our pickup truck. My father had just spent about $125 for a set of new tires and tubes and a brand new battery. So he asked for $125. The man 'bought' our pickup for $25." Opportunism wasn't limited to individuals. The government seemed to profit from sudden forced sales, too. Here is Shizuka LaGrange's recollection: "In 1941 we purchased a new Chevrolet which the army took and reimbursed us in the amount of $300."

Farmers faced the problem of deciding what to do with their crops. Tom C. Clark, chief of the civilian staff, Western Defense Command, wrote, "There can be no doubt that all persons who wish to show their loyalty to this country should continue farming operation to the fullest extent."[9] Failure to care for crops would be considered an act of sabotage. Yet, when a strawberry grower asked for a twenty-four-hour extension on his evacuation notice so that he could harvest his crop, the request was denied. He plowed under the plants, strawberries and all. The next day he was picked up by the FBI on the charge of sabotage, and jailed.[10]

The Japanese American Citizens League urged Japanese nationals and Japanese Americans to cooperate with the evacuation. The feeling was that the best way to demonstrate their loyalty to the United States was to do whatever the government ordered. "*Shikata ga nai*" was a phrase whispered over and over. It means both "It cannot be helped" and "It must be done." The ethnic Japanese had but a small voice in America and no representation in Washington, D.C. Outnumbered, they lived in a climate of pervasive fear and overt racism. And so the majority of them complied with the orders.

The exclusion orders did not go completely unprotested, however. There were both small and large challenges. Joe Yamamoto put "an ad in our local paper stating that I wanted to dispose of a car, a 1941, which had three brand new tires with it. These were premium items in those days. I gave an address that was fictitious. They could go chase around the block for a few times." John Kimoto was tempted to burn down his house: "I

38

went to the storage shed to get the gasoline tank and pour the gasoline on my house, but my wife ... said don't do it, maybe somebody can use this house; we are civilized people, not savages."

Others sought justice through the courts. Mary Ventura, a Japanese American married to a Filipino, filed a habeas corpus petition to challenge the curfew. Her petition was denied, however, because she had not violated the curfew and therefore was not entitled to the release from custody that a habeas corpus provides.[11]

Minoru Yasui, a Japanese American and a reserve officer in the army, was employed by the consulate general of Japan at the time of Pearl Harbor. When news of the attack reached the mainland, he immediately resigned his consular position and sought active duty in the military. The army turned him away. Later he deliberately violated the curfew to get himself arrested in order to test its constitutionality. The district judge hearing Yasui's case agreed that the curfew was unconstitutional as applied to American citizens, but upheld Yasui's arrest. The judge decided that Yasui had renounced his birthright citizenship by having worked for the Japanese consulate![12]

Another Nisei, Fred Korematsu, was planning to marry a Caucasian woman when the evacuation orders were announced. He defied the orders by changing his name, altering his appearance through plastic surgery, and going into hiding. The FBI arrested him in a prohibited zone, and Korematsu defended himself on the basis that the evacuation orders were unconstitutional.[13]

American-born university student Gordon Hirabayashi also tested the legality of DeWitt's proclamations. He was arrested for violation of the curfew imposed by Military Public Proclamation No. 1.[14] His case, like those of Minoru Yasui and Fred Korematsu, was taken to the Supreme Court of the United States. Sadly, in all three cases the Court ruled in December 1944 that the curfew and exclusion were constitutional in a time of military necessity, though it did restore Yasui's citizenship.

On the same day in December 1944 that the Supreme Court upheld the government's right to establish a curfew and exclusion policy during a time of military necessity, it ruled in the case of Mitsuye Endo, a twenty-two-year-old stenographer for the state of California who had been evacuated to Tule Lake. Endo charged that the government had no right to detain loyal citizens in the camps. In this case, the Court sidestepped the constitutional issues of the evacuation by addressing the WRA's leave policy. Justice William O. Douglas wrote that the WRA had no power to subject loyal citizens to a "leave procedure."[15] On one hand, the Supreme Court upheld the evacuation orders. On the other, however, it denied the right of the government to hold loyal Japanese Americans in the camps.

Before the Endo ruling came down, though, the majority of Japanese nationals and American-born citizens of Japanese ancestry, directed by one of 108 Civilian Exclusion Orders, had received their family numbers and reported to buses and trains for the first leg of their journey. They were told little about where they were going, and they were allowed to take with them only what they could carry. "So much we left behind," said Teru Watanabe, "but the most valuable thing I lost was my freedom." Another evacuee, Betty Matsuo, said, "I lost my identity. At that time, I didn't even have a Social Security number, but the WRA gave me an I.D. number. That was my identification."

Beyond knowing which of the sixteen assembly centers they were to report to, the evacuees were unaware of their ultimate destinations. They didn't know if they eventually would be relocated to desert or mountain or swamp. They knew only the official WRA line: that they were going to "land that was raw, untamed, and full of

40

opportunities" (quoted in *Justice Denied*). Their future was clouded in uncertainty. What awaited them was anybody's guess.

Grace Nakamura recalled her trip: "On May 16, 1942 ... we departed ... for an unknown destination. To this day, I can remember vividly the plight of the elderly, some on stretchers, orphans herded onto the train by caretakers, and especially a young couple with four preschool children. The mother had two frightened toddlers hanging on to her coat. In her arms she carried two crying babies. The father had diapers and other baby paraphernalia strapped to his back. In his hands he struggled with duffel bag and suitcase. The shades were drawn on the train for our entire trip. Military police patrolled the aisles."

Sumiko Seo Seki and her family were evacuated to Santa Anita Assembly Center. "We were only allowed to take with us just what we could carry. We left the crops that were about to be harvested in the field. ... We tried to sell our things for whatever we could get. In the confusion, many people simply walked off with our things. ... Hardly anything was ready for us when we arrived ... [at Santa Anita]. We slept in a stable only recently vacated by horses. The first day we were given a sack to fill with straw for our mattress. The smell of the animals never seemed to leave us."

Only upon entry into the assembly centers did many evacuees fully realize the extent to which their individual rights, those rights "guaranteed" under the Constitution of the United States of America and its Bill of Rights, were being suspended. William Kochiyama was sent to Tanforan Assembly Center near San Francisco. He told this story: "At the entrance ... stood two lines of troops with rifles and fixed bayonets pointed at the evacuees as they walked between the soldiers to the prison compound."

Jim Kawaminami recalled his entry into one assembly center: "The day of the evacuation many of us were first sent to assembly centers, which were either fairgrounds or racetracks, taking with us only those things we were able to carry. Surrounded by barbed-wire fences and guard towers, we were assigned living quarters. Many of the families were put into horse stables which were very unsanitary and the stench was unbearable."

The sight of armed troops, guard towers, and barbed-wire fences became firmly etched in the minds of most evacuees. One of the army's arguments in support of the evacuation and relocation was that exclusion would protect the ethnic Japanese from angry mobs of Caucasian citizens. In truth, some bigoted individuals set fire to Japanese-owned businesses and threw rocks at their houses, but these incidents were minor compared to the picture painted by the army. Mary Sakaguchi Oda came to realize that "democracy can be an illusion and constitutional rights a meaningless phrase.... There are some ... who say that we were there for our protection. If so, why were the guns pointed toward us rather than away from us?"

War is always a time of limited supplies, and World War II was no exception. The shortage of labor and lumber meant that evacuees arrived at hastily converted assembly centers that were often unfinished and offered only spartan accommodations. At Pinedale, for example, Ken Hayashi remembered that the "camp consisted of tar paper–roofed barracks with gaping cracks that let in insects" and that there were "no toilet facilities except smelly outhouses." James T. Fujii was sent to the Portland stockyard where "roughly two thousand people [were] packed in one large building. No beds were provided, so they gave us gunny sacks to fill with straw, that was our bed." The heat left a vivid impression on Thomas M. Tajiri. He described Santa Anita this way: "In the hot summers, the legs of the cots were

42

sinking through the asphalt." And always there was the constant reminder of the presence of the military. "It had extra guard towers with a searchlight panoraming [*sic*] the camp," said Marshall Sumida about Santa Anita.

Many former evacuees remembered the food. Often accustomed to seafood, garden-fresh vegetables, and rice, some were forced to make dietary changes when they first entered the assembly centers. Breakfast, consisting of eggs or bacon and coffee or tea, was tolerable, but the other meals sometimes matched the spartan housing. Shizuko Tokushige recollected lunch and dinner as "an ice cream scoop of rice, a cold sardine, a weeny, or sauerkraut." James Goto could not forget that for "the first few months our diet . . . consisted of brined liver—salted liver. Huge liver. Brown and bluish in color . . . [that] would bounce if dropped." Eventually the evacuees took over menu planning and food preparation. Who could blame them?

The War Civil Control Administration conceived of the assembly centers as temporary housing, but the construction of the more permanent relocation centers took longer than anticipated. Instead of providing shelter for a few weeks, assembly centers became "home" for many evacuees for months. As summer approached, it became apparent that some semblance of a normal life would have to be provided. Rudimentary schools were set up, staffed by evacuees. Recreation was organized, and religious services were offered. Masaaki Hironaka described a "standard round of jobs, from doctor to janitor." Each assembly center, surrounded by barbed wire, became a self-contained community.

General DeWitt established the official wage scale. At a time when wages were considerably higher on the outside, unskilled Japanese American workers in the assembly centers received $8.00 a month and skilled workers earned $12.00 a month. Professional people, like doctors and teachers, were paid an incredible

$16.00 a month. At the time, Caucasian teachers and librarians hired by the WRA earned around $2,000 a year. The internees protested this disparity, but civilians outside the camps loudly voiced their own opinions and argued that wages for evacuees should not exceed a soldier's base pay of $21 a month. Once again the vocal majority won out.

And everywhere there was supervision. Religious services were monitored for fear they might be used for propaganda. Center newspapers were allowed to carry only items that the Wartime Civil Control Administration had cleared.[16] Armed military police patrolled the perimeters of the assembly centers and manned the guard towers, while an internal police force composed of deputized evacuees took care of matters inside the barbed wire.[17]

Life in the assembly centers differed from life outside in another way, too. Visits to the camps were controlled, as they are in prison. Some visitors arrived with cakes and pies, only to have them cut in half to ensure that they contained no weapons or contraband. Some assembly centers permitted evacuees and visitors to speak only through a wire barrier. At others, each family was issued only one visitor's permit a week, and the visit was limited to thirty minutes.[18]

Sumiko Seo Seki spent a total of six months at Santa Anita. She summed up her assembly center experience this way: "[It was] ... my first lesson in prejudice." But Sumiko and most other evacuees—the majority of whom were American citizens and all of whom were deprived of their privacy and freedom—quietly accepted their condition. *Shikata ga nai.* It cannot be helped. It must be done.

They hoped the next leg of their journey would be better. Toward the end of May 1942, evacuees again began to line up. This time they were transferred to the relocation centers, American-style concentration

44

camps. "As I passed my high school," remembered Sally Tsuneishi, "I saw the American flag waving in the wind, and my emotions were in a turmoil. I thought of the prize-winning essay that I had written for my high school English class and it was entitled 'Why I Am Proud to Be an American.' As tears streamed down my face, an awful realization dawned on me: I am a loyal American, yet I have the face of an enemy."

- 5 -
"EVEN GOD IN HEAVEN IS CRYING FOR US"

"The day we left for camp, it was at a bus stop in Burbank on a very gray, cloudy day," remembered Mary Sakaguchi Oda, "and just before we got on the bus, it began to rain. The mother of two standing next to me said, 'See, even God in heaven is crying for us.'"

While a few traveled in private automobiles accompanied by armed military guards, the majority of evacuees made the journey to the relocation centers by train or bus. Some were loaded like cattle into open military trucks and transported to their destinations. Those who were able to travel by private automobile were the luckiest, according to Mabel T. Ota. She explained that she and her husband sold their car to "a young man who worked at a neighborhood gas station, and he agreed to drive us to Poston [Arizona]. We did have an advantage in that we could load up the car with many personal belongings, including pots, pans, and my sister Margaret's sewing machine." Other evacuees were limited once again to what they could carry.

Not all of the relocation centers were in the desert, but Henry McLemore's dream of giving the evacuees "the inside room in the badlands" came true. All of the camps were deliberately isolated. Rumors abounded, and many feared that the government would simply abandon them to wander aimlessly in barren interior

46

lands, much as it had done with the Native Americans. One evacuee related this story: "[M]y mother purchased canteens for water containers, high boots to protect us from rattlesnakes, and heavy canvas to be made into bags to carry our belongings. . . . The irony was we were sent . . . to Rohwer, Arkansas, which has more swamps than desert."

One rumor conflicted with the next, and evacuees were uneasy. The journey itself did little to soothe their emotions. Often their trains waited motionless on sidings as freight trains with higher priority passed. Delays were sometimes as long as ten hours. The trains were crowded and uncomfortable, and most evacuees had to sit up during the entire trip. Charlie Hamasaki boarded a train at Union Station in Los Angeles. "When we walked in [to the train], they told us to pull all the blinds down." Of course, this military order made an already uncomfortable train stifling, because adequate ventilation was impossible. It also increased the despair that evacuees were feeling. Young Charlie was an inquisitive lad, though. "For four days we traveled. During that time . . . they asked me, the Issei old men, 'Where are we going?' When I peeked, it was Fresno. . . . The next thing I know it was Stockton, Sacramento, Redding, Portland. . . ."

Arthur Tsuneishi had been taught "to be obedient to parents, to superiors, your country. Thus, we complied to this order [and were] herded meekly as lambs into an American concentration camp." There remains controversy over the contention that the relocation centers were actually concentration camps, a term first used to denote detention facilities in South Africa during the Boer War of 1899–1902.[1] After World War II, the term became associated with the Nazi death camps in Europe. While American relocation centers were bleak and bare, they were not extermination camps. Yet, it must be remembered that government documents at the time, and even President Roosevelt, referred to them as concentration camps.[2]

After their long journey, some evacuees faced more harassment when they reached the concentration camps—the relocation centers. At times even the military guards theoretically assigned to protect the evacuees were the harassers. George Kasai told this story: "When we finally reached our destinations, four of us men were ordered by the military personnel carrying guns to follow them. We were directed to unload the pile of evacuees' belongings from the boxcars to the semi-trailer truck to be transported to the concentration camp. During the interim, after filling one trailer-truck and waiting for the next to arrive, we were hot and sweaty and sitting, trying to conserve our energy, when one of the military guards standing with his gun, suggested that one of us should get a drink of water at the nearby water faucet and try to make a run for it so he could get some target practice."

When Shizuko Tokushige arrived at Parker, Arizona, she was contemplating how to make the transfer from train to bus for the final leg of her journey to Poston Relocation Center. "A soldier said, 'Let me help you, put your arm out.' He proceeded to pile everything on my arm. And to my horror, he placed my two-month-old baby on top of the stack. He then pushed me with the butt of the gun and told me to get off the train, knowing when I stepped off the train my baby would fall to the ground. I refused. But he kept prodding and ordering me to move. I will always be thankful [that] a lieutenant checking the cars came upon us. He took the baby down, gave her to me, and then ordered the soldier to carry all our belongings to the bus and see that I was seated and then report back to him."

Few evacuees were prepared for what greeted them. When they stepped off the buses and trains, they were given an orientation booklet called *Questions and An-*

swers for Evacuees, which was prepared by the WRA. It described their new home, the relocation center, as a "pioneer community, with basic housing and protective services provided by the Federal Government, for occupancy by evacuees for the duration of the war." What lay before their eyes was another camp surrounded by barbed wire and guard towers equipped with searchlights and machine guns. "A . . . classmate of mine had told me that she had read in the papers that we were going to be placed in comfortable homes," said Mary Sakaguchi Oda. "When I looked at our new home, I was filled with dismay and disbelief."

Whether the evacuees arrived at: Rohwer, Arkansas, or Poston, Arizona; Heart Mountain, Wyoming, or Manzanar, California, the "comfortable homes" that greeted them at the ten relocation centers varied little. They were built to War Department specifications and would have been better suited to house rugged combat soldiers than families. Squat tar paper–covered barracks stretched out in orderly rows. Each building measured about 24 by 96 feet and was divided into rooms for individual families. A family of four was typically allowed a space measuring 24 by 20 feet.

There was no running water in the barracks. Community showers, bathrooms, and laundry facilities occupied the alley between the rows of buildings. Meals were prepared and eaten in mess halls.

These "comfortable homes" had no inside walls or ceilings, though they were "furnished." Canvas cots, a light bulb hanging overhead, and a potbellied stove were standard.

Evacuees were left with different impressions of the relocation centers. One compared Tule Lake Relocation Center to the Arboga Assembly Center this way: "[Tule Lake] had running water in the toilets and the bathtubs and showers. All these facilities had individual stalls. This was like leaving the flophouses and moving to the

49

Ritz." But another described the bathroom accommodations at Poston Relocation Center this way: "Using the bathroom and showers in the community fashion was unpleasant. The toilets were partitioned, but [had] no door in front. No privacy for the most intimate matters." Yet another recalled Minidoka Relocation Center in Idaho: "When we first arrived at Minidoka, everyone was forced to use outhouses since the sewer system had not been built. For about a year, the residents had to brave the cold and the stench of these accommodations."

The WRA dared not make life too comfortable for the evacuees. Civilian watchdog groups were adamant that harsh camps were fair retaliation for Pearl Harbor and Japan's continuing victories. But the evacuees were resourceful. They used what few materials were available to improve their accommodations and make life at least tolerable. They turned scrap lumber into furniture and began to fashion parks from land that once stood barren. For other items, they saved and pooled their monthly wages and placed orders through the Sears Roebuck catalog.

All of the evacuees were unprepared for the weather, which varied from camp to camp. Dust, however, seemed to be a universal component. Monica Sone wrote this about her first day at Minidoka: "Our first day of camp, we were given a rousing welcome by a dust storm. . . . We felt as if we were standing in a gigantic sand-mixing machine as the sixty-mile gale lifted the loose earth up into the sky, obliterating everything. Sand filled our mouths and nostrils and stung our faces and hands like a thousand darting needles."[3] Lawrence Yatsu, a high school senior, described Poston: "The earth around Poston is not unlike parched flour; it is fine dust which the wind blows around readily."[4] In fact, evacuees had special nicknames for the three separate camps that made up Poston: Roaston, Toaston, and

Duston. These offered a vivid and accurate description of the harsh Arizona desert surrounding Poston and hinted at a place where temperatures could soar to 115°F or 120°F in the summer.

The dust was far more than a mere nuisance. It took a physical toll on some. Mary Sakaguchi Oda described the impact on her family: "My older sister developed bronchial asthma in camp. It was a reaction to the terrible dust storms and winds. The asthma became intractable, and she died at the age of twenty-six."

Those evacuated to desert relocation centers were surprised by the heat, which challenged many to invent ways to stay cool. Kanshi Yamashita, a high school senior in Poston, wrote a composition titled "Summer in Poston or ..." In it, he paints an expressive picture: "And those hot summer days and the things we learned! Self-appointed experts in the art of keeping cool, that's what we are! Saturate the floor with water, take off all clothing, dump all available bath towels in a bucket of water, drape them on oneself à la Gandhi, and there we were, just as hot as ever."[5]

At the opposite extreme were the winters. The majority of the evacuees were from coastal California, where mild weather year-round had left them ill-equipped for the harsh winters awaiting them at some of the camps. For many, the camps provided their first experience with snow and freezing weather. That none of them froze was a miracle. Here's what Charlie Hamasaki had to say: "When we got off the train ... 25 degres below zero, man. I'm from southern California. I had my moccasins—not shoes, moccasins—with me, and just a T-shirt and overcoat. So when we got off the train [there was] a snow drift ten-foot high. [It was] cold like hell ... and they have to line us up in the freezing weather to count the heads so nobody would escape.... And we did that every morning, every morning, man, for one month."

51

Sally Tsuneishi was from Hawaii. Although most of the ethnic Japanese in Hawaii avoided being interned because of the scarcity of labor, influential Issei and their families were shipped across the Pacific where they could pose no threat to the American military. Sally Tsuneishi's father was a leader in several Japanese cultural organizations, and she recalled her journey. "After an ocean voyage [and] a long train ride across the country, we arrived at Jerome, Arkansas, on January 5, 1943. It was an especially cold winter for the Hawaiians. We were issued a sweater, a cap and mittens from the American Red Cross, and we wore them day and night."

The two camps in Arkansas, Jerome and Rohwer, left an indelible imprint on the minds of new inhabitants. Violet Kazue deCristoforo remembered, "Whenever we went out of doors to cut firewood or go to the mess hall, the latrine or the shower room we not only sank up to our ankles in the ooze, but had to be on the alert for snakes."[6] About Rohwer, Betty Matsuo had this to say: "Rohwer was a living nightmare."

In spite of the harsh environments and sterile living arrangements, the WRA did plan, at least on paper, to provide adequate medical personnel and facilities for the evacuees. Often there were too few Japanese doctors to staff the growing camps. Medical supplies and equipment were scarce and sometimes outdated.

One young Nisei doctor, James Goto, was asked to go to Manzanar as a favor to his fellow Japanese. He was asked to supervise the setup of hospital facilities and was promised that he would be its director at a stipend of about $5,000 per year, a salary not unusual for a new doctor at the time. "I accepted the challenge," James said, "and also the said stipend, but sad to say actually got $19 per month for four full years."

Afraid of being accused of coddling the evacuees, the WRA, with Milton Eisenhower at its head, adopted a wage scale of $12, $16, or $19 a month, depending on the professional and technical skills required in a job. Just as it had when the ethnic Japanese first gathered in the assembly centers, public opinion dictated that such low wages be paid in spite of protests from the evacuees. Any talk of paying the evacuees more was immediately squelched by the watchdog groups bent on making the evacuation as unpleasant as possible for a people with "the face of the enemy."

Low wages notwithstanding, James Goto had a hospital to erect, but little did he realize how great a challenge lay ahead of him. "When I arrived in Manzanar in a jeep driven by a soldier in the early part of March, there was erected on this vast desert at the base of Mt. Whitney only one kitchen [and] three tar-papered barracks.... We set up a temporary hospital with a bench-like table for operating.... On the second day after I arrived in Manzanar, toward evening the temperature dropped below freezing point. One of my younger helpers was skipping rope to keep warm.... I started to scrub my hands at the faucet. I noticed my hands turning different colors and becoming numb, and the faucets stopped running and icicles formed.... To keep the operating room ... warm was a simple pot-bellied wood stove [and] no facilities for any hot water."

Over time, the medical facilities improved at the various camps. But available supplies often left much to be desired. James remembered when "two carloads of 1918 cotton bandages, old sutures, and instruments from World War I arrived." Mounting casualties from defeats in both the Pacific and Europe were straining the availability of medical supplies. Military needs were given priority, followed by civilian needs. The last ones to receive medical shipments, when they were available, were the people in the camps.

In addition to shortages of medicines, overwork crippled the staff and diminished its ability to provide proper care. One of the most heartrending stories was told by Mabel T. Ota. She and her husband Fred were just starting their married life when the war burst upon them and they were evacuated to Poston: "By the latter part of 1942, the administration began encouraging people to leave camp if they could find a sponsor. Fred was offered a job in New York by the Quakers as assistant manager of cooperative distributors, a mail-order house. He left camp, but I stayed behind because I was pregnant and expecting a baby in May 1943.

"The baby arrived a month early, after eight months' gestation, on April 13, 1943. When I arrived at the hospital, a nurse checked me in. She stated the doctor had delivered three babies and had collapsed, so he had returned to his barracks for a much needed rest. There was only one OB doctor [obstetrician] for the entire camp. The nurse checked me infrequently.... After twenty-eight hours of labor, the nurse became concerned.... The doctor examined me and said, 'Your baby's heartbeat is getting very faint. I will have to use forceps ... and I will have to give you a local pain killer because we do not have an anesthesiologist. We can't wait any longer because we do not have a resuscitating machine to revive the baby.'...

"After using the scalpel to cut me, he picked up the forceps. I thought it looked like the ice tongs used by the iceman when he delivered a block of ice, only the ends were long and flat, not curved and pointed.... When I saw her [the baby] after three days, I noticed a large scab on the back of her head. She has a bald spot there to this day. Madeline is a developmentally disabled person. She is mentally retarded and has grand mal epileptic [seizures].... Many, many times I have wished that Madeline could have been born by caesarean operation. She [might] then have been a normal, whole person."

By the fall of 1942, some 106,770 evacuees had been relocated. Where once only deserts and swamps had existed, full-scale communities now bustled behind barbed wire. That summer, the evacuees had celebrated the Fourth of July with red, white, and blue streamers like any average American community. Now adults went off to work at community newspapers, cooperative farming enterprises, camouflage net factories, and other businesses that provided goods and services to the evacuees or contributed to the war effort. Children wandered off to school to pledge allegiance to the flag before tackling the three *R*'s.

Paul Chikahisa described his school at Poston: "We had classes in barracks, no playground, and some of the most inadequate teachers. . . . I felt . . . that the older teachers must have been rejects from other schools, and that the young ones were interested only in having a good time with the military police." Seating was at a premium, with students typically occupying the floor until chairs and desks could be salvaged from other school districts or built from scrap lumber. At Tule Lake, typing classes had no typewriters. James Hirabayashi recalled that he and the other students "drew circles on a sheet of paper, lettered the circles, and practiced by pressing our fingers over the circles."

Still, life was beginning to take on a semblance of normalcy. Yet under the surface, tensions were rising. The strong, cohesive unity that had characterized the Japanese family was breaking down as a result of community mess halls. Pro-American and pro-Japanese factions began to form in the camps, and members began to voice their differences. The pro-Japanese groups were largely composed of evacuees who were openly resentful of their treatment. Members of one such group, the Fair Play Committee, actively protested their

55

treatment, and their actions resulted in federal prison sentences. Also, a rift was beginning to develop between the Issei and the Nisei. The older men had traditionally set standards and rules, but this tradition was lost as a result of WRA regulations that forbade the Issei to sit on any community committee. Suddenly the Issei were being dictated to by their American-born children.

As tensions grew at some camps, various factions jockeyed for power. Small riots erupted at Poston and Manzanar, as labels of "informer" and "collaborator" were pinned on pro-American individuals. There were other problems as well. Evacuees suspected some WRA personnel of stealing food from the warehouses and selling it on the black market or selling it to the internees at inflated prices. There were strikes and pickets, and the WRA began to look for ways to hasten the return of the evacuees to society.

From the outset, a few evacuees would be released from the relocation centers to harvest crops or continue their college education. By the summer of 1942, farmers feared that crops would be lost. They petitioned the White House for help, and the agricultural leave program began. In addition to paying evacuees prevailing wages, employers were required to provide housing outside of the camps. The Japanese laborers were hard-working and efficient; they not only earned the respect of their employers but also were credited with saving the sugar beet crop in the western states.[7]

In large part, the agricultural leave program was successful, and evacuees were given an opportunity to earn more than they could have if they had remained in the relocation centers. Nonetheless, conditions weren't always as promised. George Taketa was led by a farm supervisor "to a large horse barn, one-third of which was filled with hay. He told us this was where we were going to sleep." Others found that their housing was, at best, only rudimentary. "Our living quarters was a shack

56

without running water, heated by a coal stove," recalled John Takashi Omori, "and we had to bathe in a ditch."

There were also a few incidents of hostility from the communities in which the laborers worked. One evacuee reported being arrested and beaten by police while traveling back to Poston. Another described how local hooligans made teenage evacuees crawl through a city park.

Some of the evacuees were college students, whose forced evacuation interrupted their studies. Efforts were made to transfer them to other institutions outside the Western Defense Command, but there was resistance. One early rule forbade students to attend a school within twenty-five miles of a railroad. Another prohibited Nisei students from attending any college that was even remotely connected with the war effort. Thus colleges and universities with ROTC programs were off limits. Mary Sakaguchi Oda, whose medical studies were interrupted, told this story: "When I heard that they were allowing students out of camp, I applied to ... ninety-one medical schools, all but the four on the West Coast. When I received the replies, several of them stated that they could not consider my application because they had military installations on their campus. The implication of my return address—Manzanar—was that I was a potential spy or saboteur." Mary did finally gain acceptance to a women's medical school in Pennsylvania that had no connection with the military. Other students faced similar obstacles in trying to gain admission to colleges located far outside the Western Defense Command, but several religious organizations and especially the American Friends Service Committee (AFSC), a Quaker group, assisted them. Eventually more than four thousand students were able to leave the relocation centers to continue their studies.[8]

The AFSC was also instrumental in expanding the release program. With the success of the agricultural

57

and student leave programs, and with the approval of the WRA's new director, Dillon Myer, who replaced Milton Eisenhower, the AFSC found jobs for the evacuees and opened a hostel in Chicago to house some of them. Release and resettlement became a WRA priority.

Then came the Supreme Court's decision in the Endo case, which in effect *required* the WRA to release the evacuees. Government officials quickly turned their attention to how and when to comply with the ruling.

Meanwhile, the Nisei were making increased demands to be allowed to serve their country. In the hysteria surrounding Pearl Harbor and the subsequent evacuation of the ethnic Japanese from the West Coast, all Japanese males had been classified 4-C (enemy aliens). This made them unacceptable for military duty. The Japanese American Citizens League pressed for a change in policy.

In early 1943 the tide of opinion began to shift. Some officials in the government supported the formation of a Nisei combat team, although General DeWitt remained steadfast in his distrust of Japanese Americans. Even President Roosevelt took up the cause:

> *No loyal citizen of the United States should be denied the democratic right to exercise the responsibilities of his citizenship, regardless of his ancestry. The principle on which this country was founded and by which it has always been governed is that Americanism is a matter of the mind and heart; Americanism is not, and never was, a matter of race or ancestry. A good American is one who is loyal to this country and to our creed of liberty and democracy. Every loyal American citizen should be given the opportunity to serve this country wherever his skills will make the greatest contribution—whether it be in the ranks of our armed forces, war production, agriculture, government service, or other work essential to the war effort.[9]*

To expedite the resettlement and the formation of a Nisei fighting group, the government sent to evacuees age seventeen and older a questionnaire in the first weeks of 1943. The purpose of the questionnaire was to determine the loyalty of internees, but it contained two questions that caused a stir.[10] Question 27 asked: "Are you willing to serve in the armed forces of the United States on combat duty, wherever ordered?" Question 28 asked: "Will you swear unqualified allegiance to the United States of America and faithfully defend the United States from any and all attack by foreign and domestic forces, and forswear any form of allegiance or obedience to the Japanese emperor, or any other foreign government, power or organization?"

The government gave little thought to the implications of the questions. To be considered loyal, an evacuee was expected to answer yes to both of them. But most Issei at that time were too old to serve in the military and were ineligible for other reasons. Many suspected that question 27 was some sort of government trick. By far the most controversy, however, surrounded question 28. An affirmative answer to this question would have called upon the Issei to renounce the only citizenship they had. They were barred by law from becoming citizens of the United States, and so an affirmative answer made them people without a country. Some Nisei, on the other hand, wondered if an affirmative answer to question 28 forswearing their allegiance to the Japanese emperor was an admission that such an allegiance had once existed.[11]

Albert Nakai was one who answered no to both questions: "Well, I am one of those that said 'no, no' on [the questionnaire], one of the 'no, no' boys, and it is not that I was proud about it, it was just that our legal rights were violated and I wanted to fight back.... It just got me so damned mad." Another no-no boy, Chiyoji Iwao, explained his reason: "I answered both questions number 27 and 28 in the negative, not because of disloyalty but due to the disgusting and shabby treatment given us."

The Fair Play Committee (FPC) squared off against the Japanese American Citizens League (JACL) on the issue of the questionnaire. The JACL encouraged evacuees to answer both questions affirmatively and recommended that Nisei males should volunteer for the draft as a way of demonstrating their loyalty. The FPC, however, was outraged at the questionnaire and angered at the incarceration of Japanese Americans. The FPC maintained that their loyalty should never have been at issue in the first place. They encouraged a negative response to both questions and overtly opposed the draft.

Other people refused outright to answer either question. Families divided over the issue. Still, confusion notwithstanding, most answered yes to both questions. Mary Sakaguchi Oda explained that her family "all wrote 'yes, yes.' There is a Japanese saying, '*umi-no-oya-yori mo sodate no oya*,' meaning 'your adoptive parents are your real parents.' "

With loyalty verified, some applied for leave from the camps and set off to rebuild the life they had lost and to help with the civilian war effort. Many others, unsure of attitudes on the outside, remained in camp. Though for many internees the reasons for answering no had little to do with loyalty, all who answered no to questions 27 and 28 were transferred to Tule Lake for continued confinement.

Other young Nisei men and women who felt an obligation to serve their country volunteered for America's military. Mitsuo Usui recalled that it was the first disagreement he'd had with his father: "When the Nisei combat battalion was being formed, I volunteered and had my first fallout with my father. He thought that after all the hardship created by the incarceration of our

60

people, I had the nerve even to think of joining up with the armed forces. 'We lose everything—the property, the business, our home,' Papa said. 'It's like kicking you in the pants and then now they're saying come in and shine my shoes.' But I explained that it was my duty to volunteer as a citizen of this country, and as a citizen I must fight for our country and even die for it. He kicked me out of the barracks. I slept in the furnace room that night because I dared not go back and feared going back to the barrack unit where we were staying. It was my mother that came to me the next day and said, 'If you feel that strongly about your country, then you volunteer and go.... I'll take care of Papa.' "

Mitsuo joined thousands of Nisei men and women who were eager to prove their loyalty and gain the safe release of their families from America's concentration camps. To restore their dignity and respect, they put on the uniform of the government which had denied them their freedom and went to war.

– 6 –
"TO BECOME 'EQUALS' WITH OTHERS"

"They were ordinary youths wanting to live, but they became 'extraordinary' as they dared to choose to come forth from the concentration camps to fight for the land that had incarcerated them and their families. And they became heroes because they dared to take that first step to become 'equals' with others in American society. They stood apart and were not dismayed or dissuaded by forces that weighed against them." So wrote Captain George Aki, chaplain to the Nisei fighting unit that was formed when the military lifted its ban on Japanese American volunteers.[1]

Some 33,000 Nisei served in the military during World War II.[2] Most of them came from the relocation centers, and they left family and friends behind the barbed-wire fences to prove their allegiance to America and its democratic ideals.

Oddly, the new volunteers weren't the first Nisei to serve in America's military during the war. At the time of the attack on Pearl Harbor, a number of Nisei were already in military service to their country. Because of widespread distrust following the attack, however, the War Department discharged many of them. In spite of these actions, two groups remained intact: the Military Intelligence Service Language School (MISLS) and the 100th Battalion.

The MISLS was begun by two forward-thinking military officers, Lieutenant Colonel John Weckerling and Captain Kai Rasmussen.[3] Early in 1941 they had argued that specialists in the Japanese language might be useful if the United States and Japan continued on a collision course. After winning approval in November 1941, they started a small language school in the San Francisco area with four Nisei instructors and sixty students, fifty-eight of whom were Japanese Americans.

Weckerling's and Rasmussen's actions proved to be prophetic when Japan attacked Pearl Harbor on December 7, 1941. Ironically, the MISLS fell victim to the army's own restrictions. When General DeWitt issued the evacuation orders in the spring of 1942, the school was quickly transferred away from the West Coast—to Minnesota! This irony didn't go unnoticed by the Japanese Americans. As Mark Murakami explained, "[On] the one hand the Japanese Americans were condemned for having the linguistic and cultural knowledge of Japanese, and on the other hand the knowledge they had was capitalized on and used as a secret weapon by the Army and Navy Intelligence."

By the time the school closed in 1946, it had trained more than six thousand men.[4] During its existence, the linguists, usually working in teams, translated captured documents and intercepted messages. This enabled American commanders to anticipate Japanese maneuvers and plan counterstrikes. MIS language specialists took part in every major campaign in the Pacific, and General Douglas MacArthur's intelligence chief credited the MISLS with shortening the war by two years and averting one million U.S. casualties.[5] After Japan's surrender, the MISLS shifted its focus to the American military occupation of Japan, where linguists interpreted for U.S. military teams and helped to locate and repatriate imprisoned Americans.

The 100th Battalion, the other unit that had remained intact, hailed from Hawaii. The attack on Pearl Harbor had spawned fear and distrust of Japanese nationals and Japanese Americans living in Hawaii. They were 3,000 miles closer to the enemy than their mainland counterparts, and yet their constitutional rights were upheld to a greater degree than were those of Japanese Americans in the Western Defense Command.[6] In Hawaii, Japanese nationals and Japanese Americans were a source of scarce labor. There were no calls for mass evacuation and internment.

While General Delos C. Emmons, commander of the army in Hawaii, mustered the Japanese Americans out of the Hawaiian Territorial Guard, his actions were less swift toward the Nisei serving in the National Guard. Before Emmons could discharge them, the military governor's office recommended that the Nisei be allowed to continue their service. Also, a group calling itself the Varsity Victory Volunteers, made up of veterans discharged from the Hawaiian Territorial Guard, offered to serve in any capacity in the army. Impressed with the desire of so many Hawaiian Nisei to demonstrate their loyalty to the United States, General Emmons reversed his decision and lobbied for a special Nisei battalion. He also recommended that the Nisei battalion be trained on the mainland, for fear that if another Japanese attack occurred, the Nisei might be mistaken for the enemy.[7] On June 10, 1942, the Hawaiian Provisional Battalion—soon to become the 100th Battalion—sailed into Oakland, California. From there, the group was transported by train to Camp McCoy, Wisconsin, for training.[8]

The men of the 100th trained from June to December. That winter was the first time that many of the Hawaiians had seen snow, but neither heat nor cold deterred them from performing at their peak. Indeed they were earning medals even before their training was complete, receiving five soldier's medals for rescuing a

*Japanese-Americans arrive at the assembly center,
where they are greeted by military guards
and barbed wire.*

*The suitcase belonging to this couple is being
searched for radios, cameras, and other
"spying" devices.*

Barbed wire and guard towers (background, right)
surround these young Japanese-Americans who were
born in the United States.

Dust storms were one of the many difficult conditions that had to be endured at the isolated internment camps.

*This internment camp is typical of the camps
that were home to Japanese-American citizens
during the war.*

Young people tried to continue their normal activities while living in the camps, for example, having this girl scout march (above) and this high school dance (facing page).

*Nisei translators of Japanese and English
contributed to shortening the war and reducing
casualties among American soldiers.*

Occupants of the camps performed many different jobs. Here is a watchmaker at work with a poster for United States Defense Bonds in the background demonstrating his loyalty.

The Nisei fighting units earned more military honors
than any other group in American history. While their
relatives were imprisoned in the internment camps,
these Japanese-American forces fought in the military
campaign in Italy.

A Nisei soldier in uniform visits his family living in an American-style concentration camp.

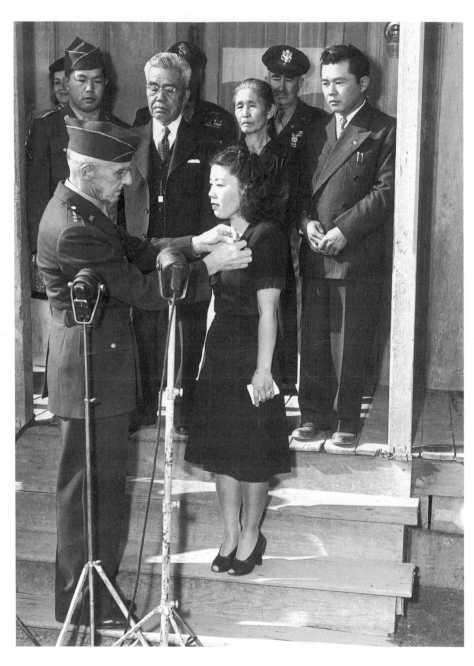

General Joseph Stilwell presents the Distinguished Service Cross to Mary Masuda, the sister of Sergeant Kazuo Masuda.

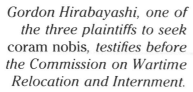

Disillusioned resident aliens seek repatriation to Japan.

Gordon Hirabayashi, one of the three plaintiffs to seek coram nobis, *testifies before the Commission on Wartime Relocation and Internment.*

The family of Minoru Yasui testifies. Yasui died before the appeal of his World War II conviction was reversed.

Attorney General Richard Thornburgh presents reparation checks to the eldest survivors of the internment.

The camp cemetery at Manzanar remains as a silent testiment to the internment of Japanese-Americans whose rights were violated by the U.S. government.

group of civilians who almost drowned in a frozen lake.[9] Later the group was transferred to Camp Shelby in Mississippi, where it met up with the newly formed 442nd Regimental Combat Team.

Many of the Nisei in the 442nd had come from the concentration camps—the relocation centers; others came from Hawaii, the Midwest, the North, and the South. All of them had been classified 4-C (enemy alien), by the Selective Service, and they were out to prove their loyalty.

The original 442nd patch, designed by the War Department, depicted a yellow arm brandishing a red sword. It was received with little enthusiasm, and the 442nd set about designing a patch that would reflect the true spirit of their team. Eventually, thanks to the efforts of the 442nd's Mitch Miyamoto, a new design was agreed to: a silver arm and hand thrusting a torch against a field of blue surrounded by a silver and red border.[10] It represented the freedom and liberty that these former evacuees were struggling for.

A little over a year after arriving on the mainland, the 100th was combat ready and ordered to North Africa. Almost immediately, the battalion left North Africa and went north to Italy, going into combat at Salerno.[11]

While the 100th fought its way up the Italian peninsula, the 442nd trained in Camp Shelby, at first using toy guns instead of real weapons. Commanding officers, who were slow to trust the Nisei volunteers, secretly opened and read letters volunteers had written back to relatives in the relocation centers. These letters convinced the commanders that trust in the 442nd was warranted, and real guns and ammunition were issued to them. By May 1944, the outfit was ready for combat and sailing toward an unknown destination. Two weeks into their journey, the 442nd's destination became clear when its members were given a booklet of Italian phrases.[12] On June 2, 1944, the battalion landed at Naples and pushed on to a staging area near the beaches of Anzio. Almost immediately, the 442nd came under fire as German airplanes raided nearby ammunition dumps.

On June 15 the 442nd once again met up with the 100th.[13] By this time, the 100th had suffered over 900 casualties.[14] The combined 100th and 442nd spent the rest of summer engaged in bitter battle against the enemy as they made their way into France.

In the fall the outfit was ordered to reach the "Lost Battalion," a unit that had been cut off and isolated on a ridge in the Vosges Mountains of France. For six days the 100th-442nd battled fortified German troops, forbidding terrain, and inclement weather. They accomplished their mission, but at no small price. The 100th-442nd combat team suffered more than 800 casualties in that one week, and the fighting wasn't over.[15]

After pushing on for ten more days they drove the Germans from the ridge that had been the Lost Battalion's original objective. Moreover they took the offensive, moving the Germans off the forward slope and over the hill, opening the way for the allied forces' drive to the Rhineland.[16] The rescue of the Lost Battalion was the 100th-442nd's bloodiest battle. In less than four weeks of fighting, the casualty list numbered 2,000, of whom 140 had been killed.[17]

After a relatively quiet winter, the 100th-442nd was ordered into combat again in the spring of 1945. This time their objective was a line of ridges in the Apennines mountains in Italy. As the 100th-442nd charged into the area, Pfc Sadao S. Munemori rushed forward under heavy enemy fire to lob grenade after grenade into a machine-gun nest, eventually knocking out both guns. As he worked his way back to join his squad, an enemy grenade fell into a shell crater where two of his squad members had taken cover. He threw himself on top of the grenade, saving his two buddies at the cost of his own life. For his heroic efforts, Pfc Munemori was awarded the highest decoration that the army could give, the Congressional Medal of Honor. It was presented to his mother. Later, the *Sadao S. Munemori* became the first U.S. military ship to bear a Japanese American surname.[18]

In May the fighting in Italy was over, and by May 9 the Germans had surrendered. The 100th-442nd became the most decorated regiment in U.S. Army history. For their service in the European theater, they earned 9,486 Purple Hearts, and more than 600 were killed in action.[19] Masato Nakagawa admitted that "it was a high price to pay," but it "was to prove our loyalty which was by no means an easy [task]."

From the European theater to the Pacific theater, Nisei soldiers and Nisei WACs (women soldiers) waged two battles—one against the enemy and the other against racism. General Joseph W. Stilwell presented, posthumously, a Distinguished Service Cross to the family of Masao Masuda. On December 9, 1945, his comments were reported in the *Los Angeles Times*: "I've seen a good deal of the Nisei in service and never yet have I found one of them who didn't do his duty right up to the handle. The Distinguished Service Cross in itself is a small thing, but since it stands for gallantry in action, I hope . . . your family will remember that Sgt. Masuda, in winning it, has also won the respect and admiration of all real Americans."[20] Later, Harry Truman, who became President following the death of Franklin Delano Roosevelt, met the 100th-442nd. As he fastened the Presidential Unit banner to their regimental colors, he acknowledged their battle: "You fought not only the enemy, you fought prejudice—and you won."

But had they really won? Although the exploits of the 100th-442nd and the remarks of General Stilwell and President Truman were widely reported, prejudice

67

continued to rear its ugly head. Even as battles in Europe and the Pacific raged, Nisei soldiers on leave encountered harsh reminders of the tenuousness of their freedom. Thomas Kinada recalled his last furlough before his regiment went overseas: "I went to see my family in Heart Mountain Relocation Center. There I was for two weeks locked up once more behind barbed wire in spite of my uniform." Paul Oda "was rotated back to the States in October of 1944. I spent my furlough at the Manzanar Relocation Center where my fiancée was interned. . . . I was not allowed to leave the camp without a Caucasian escort. All I wanted to do was go to Lone Pine, a few miles away, for some provisions to celebrate our reunion. Likewise, when we went to Reno, Nevada, to be married, we were escorted by a Caucasian. . . . I was in military uniform at all times." Both fighters for democracy and freedom, Thomas and Paul were at the same time prisoners of the government they served.

Even after the war, harassment continued. Ben Hara served as a medic with the U.S. occupation forces in Japan. "One day in 1947 while serving in the hospital, a wife of an Army captain came and screamed at me without any provocation. She said, 'Get out of that uniform, you dirty Jap. You're a disgrace to my country.' Incidentally, she was a Californian."

Mitsuo Usui's story typifies the experiences of many returning veterans: "Coming home, I was boarding a bus on Olympic Boulevard. A lady sitting in the front row of the bus, saw me and said, 'Damn Jap.' Here I was a proud American soldier, just coming back with my new uniform and new paratrooper boots, with all my campaign medals and awards, proudly displayed on my chest, and this? The bus driver, upon hearing thisremark, stopped the bus and said, 'Lady, apologize to this American soldier or get off my bus.' She got off the bus."

68

General Stilwell said of the Japanese Americans, "They bought an awful hunk of America with their blood. . . . We cannot allow a single injustice to be done to the Nisei without defeating the purposes for which we fought."[21] The Nisei had fought bravely, helping to win a world war, and inroads were being made in the war against racism. It was a time for the United States to mend and heal. It was time to go home.

-7-
"I DON'T WANT ANY OF THEM HERE"

The loyalty questionnaire in the spring of 1943 and the subsequent successes of the all-Nisei fighting unit brought calls to end the exclusion. It was one thing to lock up potential enemies of the nation. But how could the incarceration of loyal residents and citizens be justified?

General DeWitt and the Western Defense Command fought against both the loyalty questionnaire and the volunteer combat unit. DeWitt feared that both of these developments might lead to the end of exclusion. He argued bitterly that "[t]here isn't such a thing as a loyal Japanese and it is just impossible to determine their loyalty by investigation—it just can't be done."[1]

Both DeWitt and Colonel Bendetsen saw an end to exclusion as an admission of wrongdoing. In voicing his opposition to the loyalty review, DeWitt commented: "I feel ... that it is a sign of weakness and an admission of an original mistake. Otherwise—we wouldn't have evacuated these people at all if we could determine their loyalty."[2] Bendetsen had another concern: "I'm scared to death principally because of the public relations part of it. That's it, to put it in a nutshell."[3] Neither officer wanted to be exposed to criticism.

On the other side were the War Department's John McCloy and Henry Stimson. While they justified the

70

evacuation on the basis that initially time had not permitted a loyalty review, they could see no valid reason to continue detention, especially of American citizens, once a loyalty review had determined their allegiance to the United States. In turn, they argued that a loyal person could hardly be considered too dangerous to return to the West Coast. In a letter to DeWitt, McCloy set forth the War Department's views: "The threat of Japanese attack is far from what it was.... [T]he War Department ... is presently looking toward the restoration of all loyal persons of Japanese ancestry ... [of] their normal rights and privileges.... I cannot help but feel that social considerations rather than military ones determine the total exclusion policy."[4]

As the loyalty review was implemented and it became clear that an end to the exclusion was at hand, DeWitt became livid with rage. Feeling that his authority had been undermined, he fired another salvo before a committee of the House of Representatives. On the topic of the ethnic Japanese returning to the West Coast, he commented: "I don't want any of them here. They are a dangerous element. There is no way to determine their loyalty."[5]

In the fall of 1943 both DeWitt and Bendetsen left the Western Defense Command. General Delos Emmons took command, and he implemented a case-by-case review process that began a return of evacuees to the West Coast at a slow trickle.[6] The exclusion had not ended, but the door to the West Coast was slowly being reopened.

It might have opened sooner and wider had it not been for the election of November 1944. When the War Department recommended that the exclusion order be rescinded, Attorney General Francis Biddle supported the move but also "doubted the wisdom of doing it at this time before the election." The President himself was reluctant "to do anything drastic or sudden." The

71

Roosevelt administration wanted another term in office and wasn't willing to risk losing it by upsetting conservative elements on the West Coast.[7] He needed the California vote.

In the days immediately following the election, however, things began to change. At its very first meeting, on November 10, the cabinet decided to revoke the exclusion order. When asked about it at a press conference toward the end of November, the president remarked that "it is felt by a great many lawyers that under the Constitution they can't be kept locked up in concentration camps."[8] And so the official exclusion came to an end and was marked by Public Proclamation No. 21 on December 17, 1944, one day before the Supreme Court's ruling in the Endo case, which outlawed the detention of loyal citizens. Still, a mass exodus from the relocation centers and back to the West Coast did not occur.

Even after the WRA scheduled closing dates for each camp, some evacuees were reluctant to leave. No matter how unpleasant the camps were, for some that life was preferable to the unknown. Many were frightened of what lay beyond the barbed wire. The WRA finally gave each remaining evacuee 25 dollars and paid the train fare for the evacuees' trip home and made them leave.

What awaited the evacuees? Many found that household items stored with neighbors and friends had been lost or stolen. Some were forced to defend their legal title to family property. Others found that their property or businesses had been taken over by former business associates or by complete strangers. Mitsuo Usui's story is probably typical of many:

The Usui family lived in . . . the southwest portion of the city of Los Angeles from 1925 until the date of the evacuation. . . . In 1938 my father and older brother,

72

my mother and younger sister started a landscape nursery on the west side of Crenshaw Boulevard just south of Country Club Drive. . . . We had enough inventory to cover almost every available space with plants on this property.

[At the time of the evacuation,] we had about two weeks, I recall, to do something—either lease the property or sell everything: the land, the building, the tools and plants. There was no way we could meet the monthly mortgage payments if we closed. In discussing this matter with my father . . . we finally decided to sell. We advertised and let the people in the neighborhood know we were selling. Finally . . . a lady . . . made an offer. She offered us $1,000 for everything—the property, the building and inventory. We took the offer because it was the best of a bad situation.

After the evacuation had ended, Mitsuo returned from his tour of military duty to Los Angeles. His father asked him to go and buy back the nursery. Mitsuo's story continued:

Still in my uniform, I hurriedly went to the nursery and asked if the owner would sell . . . [it] back to us. The owner of the nursery now was not the same person to whom we sold [it]. . . . He said, 'Yep, I'll sell you the nursery. Give me $13,000 for the land and $13,000 for the inventory.'

'Impossible!' I exclaimed, and went to the back of the property and kicked over a five-gallon can. The man wanted to know what I was doing, so I showed him some Japanese writings on the bottom of the can. 'Can you see what's written here?' I said. 'It says here this plant was planted from a seed on this date, was transplanted into a gallon-can on this date, and finally into this five-gallon can on this date. My mother

planted all these plants in the five-gallon cans and all the big trees in the back, and now you want to sell them back to us at these outrageous prices?' All he said was 'Well, that's the way the ball bounces.' I came home to tell my folks what happened. My father just broke down and cried. Thereafter my father never recovered from this incident. . . .

Starting over was especially difficult for the Issei. They were older men and women who had been looking toward retirement at the war's beginning, and now they lacked the strength, the energy, the financial resources, and even the desire to rebuild what they'd lost.

"With the help of the WRA," recalled Joyce Tamai, who was ten and a half years old at the time, "we relocated in Omaha, Nebraska, as domestic help. My father was butler and caretaker in a home in the country and my mother was cook and maid for a very nice Jewish family, whom I look back on now as having been very good people who really cared and helped.... From there, my family moved to the city. My father was a caretaker for an apartment house, and my mother was employed by a hotel as a pastry cook and later went on to become a caterer. My father would never be able to make any gains as a result of his experience in camp. My mother remembers the change in my father from the day he came home after selling his place of business to find her sitting on an apple box in the middle of an empty room. From that day, my father became—ill. My mother made all the decisions for the family from that time on. My father became progressively less able to be fully employed, and my mother . . . worked hard to keep the family together."

So embittered were some by the exclusion and internment that they returned to their native Japan. Nationwide, about eight thousand people, disillusioned and humiliated by their degrading treatment during the war years, chose to leave the United States for good.[9] A young Ben Hara became permanently separated from his family when his parents chose to repatriate to Japan rather than remain in a country that had treated them so badly. Ben, however, felt his obligation was to his own country, the United States. He remained and served proudly in America's military. His family, as he had known it, was but a memory, another victim of the exclusion and internment.

Mary Sakaguchi Oda's three surviving brothers all volunteered for America's military from the relocation centers. In response to people who ask why so many volunteered to fight for the United States after they had been treated so badly, she said, "[O]ur situation was analogous to that of battered children. We were the battered children of this country who, in spite of unspeakable treatment by their parents, still loved their motherland and fatherland and still strived to please them. Why? Because they know no other parents.

"The ones who suffered the most after the war was over were our parents. My father, when he was dying in camp, said he was going back to North Hollywood to farm again. Had he lived, he couldn't possibly have started over again at age sixty-eight. With my brother's and my father's deaths and the other members of the family not being able to support my mother, she went to work as a farm laborer, where after living in this country for thirty-four years, raising seven children, my mother—who had been a schoolteacher in Japan for seven years before coming to this country—was working on a farm doing stoop labor."

Almost without exception, evacuees left the camps to find that housing was inadequate. As the nation was preoccupied with the war effort, the limited labor force had concentrated on defeating the enemy, not on building houses and apartments. Adding complication, many Americans still harbored animosity toward the ethnic

Japanese. Some landlords refused to rent to them, and others charged them inflated prices for the most meager accommodations. Here is Sally Tsuneishi's story: "After the war, we were allowed to return to Hawaii, but there was no home for us. Our store and our home was confiscated by the plantation, and we were to start a new life in Honolulu. Without funds, the only place that we could afford was under a house—not a basement, but underneath a home. Our landlord's washtub was our bathtub, our kitchen sink, and even our laundry tub."

In most cases, every member of a family who was old enough to work had to take employment in order to make ends meet. The jobs offered required low skills and paid low wages. The government offered no assistance. John J. Saito shared this story:

> *My father first came back to Los Angeles in July of 1945, and worked as a dishwasher at a skid row restaurant on 5th Street. I came back to Los Angeles after my father and stayed at his hotel room in the skid row area. There was only one room, and only one bed, he worked the graveyard shift and I went to school during the day, therefore, we managed to use the same bed at different hours of the day. My mother was still in Idaho working as a cook at a farm labor camp. My older brother was still overseas with the 442nd Regimental Combat Team. My mother had scrimped and saved her salary as a cook for over three years, and finally had enough money for a down payment on a house. We purchased the house in 1946, and tried to move in only to find two Caucasian men sitting on the front steps with a court injunction prohibiting us from moving in because of a restrictive convenant [sic]. If we moved in, we would be subject to $1,000 fine and/or one year in the County Jail. We were in a financial bind because we could not afford both mortgage and rental payments. We*

had to sell our house during a period of a housing shortage.

In spite of all the hardships of internment and the heroic efforts of the 100th-442nd Combat Team, the ethnic Japanese still had not proven their loyalty to America—at least in the eyes of some. While alien land laws prohibited the Issei from owning property, restrictive covenants, which John mentioned above, kept the evacuees from living in certain neighborhoods. Families who managed to save up enough money for the purchase of a home in the name of a Nisei child now could not count on living in it. Even where restrictive covenants did not exist, they sometimes appeared almost overnight if a house was sold to a Nisei.

Harassment became widespread. It was common for businesses to mount anti-Japanese signs in their windows. Individuals voiced their intolerance, as Mitsuo Usui discovered when he encountered the woman on the bus who said, "Damn Jap." Even in their homes, the evacuees had to be cautious, for groups of marauding Caucasians would fire gunshots at the houses. Thirty incidents, ranging from rifle shots fired at houses to telephoned death threats, were targeted at Japanese Americans returning to California in January 1945 alone.

While the majority of those of the Issei generation never recovered their previous level of achievement, their children, the Nisei, were successful for the most part at rebuilding their lives. Joyce Tamai's story typifies most: "In 1950 we moved to our first home, which had to be in my brother's name because my parents were not citizens. I completed high school and went on to be accepted in nursing school. I was the first Japanese to be accepted in the school of nursing I attended.... I approached every task with the idea that I had to excel to prove my worth."

Even though they were now "free," those who had

been incarcerated felt a need to demonstrate their "American-ness." To prove their worth, the Nisei became a generation of achievers or, some say, overachievers.

The physical captivity was over and the arduous task of rebuilding lives had begun, but there were scars. Many Japanese Americans remained locked emotionally behind the barbed-wire fences of the concentration camps. Joyce Tamai explained:

> *I came to resent the implication that I was not as good as a non-Japanese. . . . My parents suffered the greatest loss in the camp experience. I experienced personal loss because of the disruption of home and family life, the deterioration of my father's physical and mental health, and all the bitterness, shame, anger, and hate my camp experience caused me. Depriving a child of his freedom causes personal identity problems and creates a stigma which causes shame and hatred, both of which are hard to cope with. This was a great injustice done to the Japanese citizenry of this country. . . . It should be made certain that an act of this calibre never be permitted to happen again.*

– 8 –
"THE BURDEN OF SHAME"

Although more than 120,000 people had been forced by military order into American-style concentration camps, most of the postwar generation grew up not knowing about this incarceration. The Issei were old and frail. They had little interest in reopening old wounds, and so chose not to discuss it. The Nisei, like Joyce Tamai, were too busy proving themselves by succeeding at tasks great and small. They also chose not to discuss their years at camp. Children of the Nisei, the Sansei, heard whispers about the camp experiences, but few Issei and Nisei spoke openly about them. The shame was too vast, the rejection too deeply etched. "[B]ecause of the humiliation and shame, I could never tell my four children my true feelings about that event in 1942," said Mary Sakaguchi Oda, explaining her own silence about the internment. "I did not want my children to feel the burden of shame and feeling of rejection by their fellow Americans. I wanted them to feel that in spite of what was done to us, this was still the best place in the world to live."

Over the years, the government made efforts to compensate for the exclusion and internment. In 1946, President Harry Truman signed Executive Order 9814, which pardoned 263 Nisei draft violators. Also, the first official attempt to settle property losses came with the

79

Claims Act of 1948. Without any admission of wrongdoing, the government agreed to accept claims for property losses resulting from the exclusion orders. It had, after all, promised to safeguard possessions left in the wake of evacuation. Claims totaling more than $148 million were filed. But many claims were not made. People feared harsh criticism or other governmental action. For many, silence became both a way to protect themselves and a way to deny that the internment had ever taken place.

The government, perhaps sensing that it had opened a Pandora's box, required that claims be backed up by receipts or other verifiable documents. Sadly, many of the receipts, deeds, and other papers needed to prove these claims had themselves been lost in the shuffle of the evacuation. The government paid out $37 million, a mere quarter of the amount sought.[1] Mary Sakaguchi Oda's family lost a farm. She recalled how her mother used the government's reimbursement: "She carried around the ashes of my father, brother, and sister.... When she received the government's token compensation for the family's losses, the $1,800 paid for the gravestone under which the three are now buried."

There was a loss far greater than the economic one, however. People who experience trauma sometimes repress details of the actual event. They bury the act so deep within themselves that, on the surface at least, it appears as if nothing ever happened. Inside, however, emotions boil like a caldron of witch's brew. This often causes physical and mental illness, insecurity, guilt, and shame, none of which the person has any control over. After the war, the people who had been sent away to the ten relocation centers returned to life outside the camps and began to pick up the pieces of their lives. Their camp experiences were tucked away somewhere in the deep recesses of their minds, and over time, many began to believe that their internment either hadn't really happened or had been justified. Those who felt that it was justified believed that if they were locked up like common criminals, they probably deserved it. Another group of internees, the survivors of the Nazi Holocaust, experienced a similar reaction.

As the Sansei grew older, they began to sense a gap in their cultural history. Time for their parents was measured as "pre-camp" or "after-camp," but the years spanning World War II seemed vacant. Although the Sansei asked about the camps, their questions usually went unanswered. Other times their parents might murmur, "Shikata ga nai." The feeling was that it was best not to talk about the dark years following 1942. Sue Kunitomi Embrey spoke about the emotions surrounding the internment:

> The period I spent in Manzanar was the most traumatic experience of my life. It has influenced my perspective as well as my continuing efforts to educate, persuade, and encourage others of my generation to speak out about the unspeakable crime. While speaking out has been a cathartic experience for me, I have found that it has not been the same for other former internees. In December 1969, student activists looking for an issue for the Asian-American community sponsored a pilgrimage to Manzanar. The event was widely publicized across the nation and resulted in numerous requests for information from students and a surfacing of a phenomenon which holds true today: the reluctance of the victims to discuss their experience.

Before the Commission on Wartime Relocation and Internment of Civilians on August 4, 1981, Harry Kawahara added his thoughts in an address:

81

Perhaps we can explain our situation by comparing our experience with that of a rape victim. A victim of rape is traumatized by the experience. Most rape victims find it extremely difficult to talk about it. We felt we were raped by our own country—raped of our freedom, raped of our human dignity, raped of our civil liberties. A rape victim feels guilt and shame. A victim of rape feels violated and unclean. And so it is with us. We felt that somehow we were party to this act of defilement, that we had somehow helped to bring it on. We, innocent victims, felt guilt and shame about it all. . . . It takes a long time for a rape victim to feel okay, to talk about this horrible experience. It takes a long time for the wounds to heal. . . . We have come to the realization that the camp experience had a very negative psychological effect upon us. It has profoundly affected our sense of ethnic identity and thereby, our sense of self-worth. One internee said, "I felt terribly ashamed and guilty about being Japanese.". . . Our self-esteem, our self-regard, was shattered. We did not feel comfortable talking about our camp experience with others. We scarcely talked about it with our own children. . . . It brought great discomfort to us.

But the Sansei, the children, pressed for answers to their questions. Since textbooks rarely mentioned the event, or suggested in only a brief sentence or two that the internment had been necessary, they looked to the Nisei and Issei to fill in the gaps. Not until the late 1960s and early 1970s—a time in the United States when many people began looking inward to discover their ancestral roots—did the resolve of the Sansei finally pay off. Slowly the forgotten years following 1942 started to take form as the elders began to discuss the evacuation and internment. What the Sansei found was a rich heritage, but one of a people who had silently suffered great indignities.

Speaking out about the injustices of 1942 was difficult for most. Even today, many don't speak at all of the internment. But Harry Kawahara mentioned that he and others "found that talking about our incarceration after so many years was a therapeutic experience. It was cathartic for us.... [W]e were able to get out some of these feelings—feelings of frustration, of rage, and even of anger." Japanese Americans commonly felt that they had been wronged during World War II, and they wished the government to acknowledge its guilt. With the support and encouragement of the Sansei, a grassroots movement to seek redress and reparations was organized and launched. Never before in the history of the United States had one racial group been targeted by the government for mass evacuation and incarceration in violation of their constitutional rights, and the prevailing attitude was that the government was wrong. A small but valiant group of individuals pressed the government and demanded an apology and compensation to those who had suffered.

The movement was not without its critics. The "Remember Pearl Harbor" lobby was adamantly opposed to any form of redress and reparations. They argued that the losses of the ethnic Japanese in the United States were far less significant than the American lives lost at Pearl Harbor. There is no greater sacrifice than that of a human life. But the flaw in their argument, of course, is that it places the burden of guilt for Pearl Harbor on the ethnic Japanese in America rather than on the enemy. This was an old song.

Others complained that too much time had passed, that if the Japanese American community wanted compensation, it should have taken action immediately after the war. But Harry Kawahara explained, "[I]t is not true that we simply waited.... Efforts were made in the past for relief, and some of that was obtained." Following the Claims Act of 1948, some individuals within the community had filed claims against the government for property losses resulting from the evacuation and internment, but these had been settled for a pittance or rejected outright.

A small group of committed individuals continued to work for relief, and as Harry mentioned, gains were made. In 1952, Congress reinstated Japanese American postal employees who had been dismissed from their jobs at the outbreak of the war. Also in 1952, quotas were lifted and Japanese aliens were finally granted the right to apply for United States citizenship.

In the 1970s, some Japanese Americans began to organize. In spite of the critics, the voices of the Japanese American community began to be heard through organizations like the National Coalition for Redress and Reparations and the Japanese American Citizens League. Other groups sprang up with names like Bay Area Attorneys for Redress and the Manzanar Committee. All of them worked relentlessly to have the history of Japanese Americans recognized and righted. Through their efforts, the Social Security Act of 1972 was passed, which allowed for camp time to count toward Social Security benefits. That same year, the California State Department of Parks and Recreation approved the designation of Manzanar as a historic landmark, and a year later a plaque was placed on the old stone guardhouse at the camp's entry. Its wording was a significant victory and took more than a year to negotiate:

> *In the early part of World War II, 110,000 persons of Japanese ancestry were interned in relocation centers by Executive Order No. 9066, issued on February 19, 1942.*
>
> *Manzanar, the first of ten such concentration camps, was bounded by barbed wire and guard*

84

towers, confining 10,000 persons, the majority being American citizens.

May the injustices and humiliation suffered here as a result of hysteria, racism and economic exploitation never emerge again.[2]

Then on February 19, 1976, President Gerald Ford rescinded Executive Order 9066.[3] In his Proclamation 4417, President Ford referred to the evacuation and internment as "national mistakes" and a "setback to fundamental American principles." Although Ford's proclamation was apologetic in tone, it failed to actually convey an apology or to offer amends for the losses suffered, and it certainly did nothing to erase the Supreme Court cases which upheld the military's right to suspend the Bill of Rights during a military emergency (see chapter 4).

Often led by the Sansei, Japanese Americans began to tell their stories. "We remembered the lessons we were taught in school," recalled Harry Kawahara, "about democracy, about our Constitution, about our legal rights. If you are injured, harmed, falsely imprisoned, had your character defamed, been denied your civil rights, then you seek redress. You seek restitution." And so it was. After years of lobbying by Japanese Americans, Congress, in 1980, created the Commission on Wartime Relocation and Internment of Civilians (CWRIC) and charged it with reviewing the facts and recommending remedies. It was the first major victory for Japanese Americans. Moreover, it was a testimony to the ideals of the American democracy that a group once wronged could bring their case before representatives of the very government responsible for the misdeed.

As the CWRIC was listening to testimony from more than 750 witnesses in twenty days of hearings, attorney Peter Irons, who had been combing old Justice Department files in research for a book, uncovered some enlightening documents: internal complaints by Justice Department lawyers in 1943 and 1944 that accused the government of suppressing evidence and lying before the Supreme Court in the Hirabayashi, Yasui, and Korematsu cases.[4]

To understand the significance of the Supreme Court cases and their outcome is to comprehend the feeling of betrayal that permeated the Japanese American community. Of the 120,000 internees, only Hirabayashi, Yasui, and Korematsu had taken their cases to the Supreme Court for a final judgment on the constitutionality of the evacuation and internment. These American citizens of Japanese ancestry believed the Supreme Court would strike down General DeWitt's orders. They held the conviction that no single group of American citizens could be denied liberty on the basis of ancestry alone.

Gordon Hirabayashi was a senior at the University of Washington when World War II began. When his evacuation orders came, he challenged their legality by refusing to report and was arrested for his defiance. At a one-day trial, during which U.S. District Judge Lloyd Black referred to the Japanese as "unbelievably treacherous," Gordon was convicted of violating both the curfew and the evacuation. The Supreme Court upheld both charges in June 1943.[5]

In a separate but related case, Minoru Yasui considered the curfew unlawful discrimination because it was based on ancestry and, like Gordon, he violated the order in challenge. His action brought arrest, and he was placed in solitary confinement for nine months while awaiting trial. In deciding the case, Judge James Alger Fee of the U.S. District Court in Oregon ruled that Minoru Yasui had revoked his citizenship by working for the Japanese consulate in Chicago before the war. Judge Fee wrote that the curfew was illegal as applied to American citizens, but held that Minoru Yasui was no longer a citizen. When Yasui appealed the decision to the Supreme Court in 1943, his citizenship was restored but the curfew violation was upheld.[6]

The third man, Fred Korematsu, wanted to remain with his Caucasian fiancée. When evacuation notices were posted, Fred altered his draft card and instead of evacuating had minor plastic surgery to change his appearance. On a tip, he was arrested and charged with not complying with the evacuation orders. When his case reached U.S. District Judge Adolphus F. St. Sure in San Francisco, he was convicted. His appeal to the Supreme Court in 1944 was denied.[7]

There were common threads among all three court cases. The three men were all American citizens. They believed the Constitution of the United States would serve to protect them because of their citizenship. Finally, government lawyers prosecuting the cases presented the same core of information to the justices of the Supreme Court and won judgments against each defendant.

As the highest court, the Supreme Court is the last court of appeal. Its decisions are considered final. With the Supreme Court convictions of Gordon Hirabayashi, Minoru Yasui, and Fred Korematsu, it seemed as if these judgments would forever stand as a strike against a racial group and against democratic values and ideals. Understandably, Japanese Americans felt betrayed.

But when Peter Irons uncovered Justice Department documents suggesting some irregularity in the evidence presented in the Supreme Court cases, hope was renewed. It rested in an old and seldom used legal procedure called a petition for a writ of error *coram nobis*, which, in Latin, means "error before us." In essence, *coram nobis* allows a person convicted of a crime to challenge the conviction after the sentence has been served if there was a fundamental error at the original trial.[8] At issue would be the government's claim of "military necessity" in the case of evacuation and internment.

Some forty years after the Supreme Court had upheld the decisions against Gordon Hirabayashi, Minoru Yasui, and Fred Korematsu, the three men sought another day in court. In January 1983, with Peter Irons and a group of volunteer lawyers—all of them Japanese Americans—representing them, they filed identical writs of *coram nobis* in the original trial courts in San Francisco, Portland, and Seattle. The petitions charged the government with misconduct.

Fred Korematsu's petition was the first to be heard. Victor Stone, a Justice Department lawyer, asked for a delay in the hearing until the report of the Commission on Wartime Relocation and Internment of Civilians was made public. He hinted that the CWRIC's conclusions and recommendations might settle the case. Judge Marilyn Patel agreed to the delay, giving Stone not more than sixty days after the commission's report was issued to respond to the petition.

The CWRIC released its report on June 16. The media's attention focused on the recommendation of a redress payment—$20,000 to each of the roughly 60,000 survivors of the concentration camps. The report also suggested a presidential pardon for those convicted of violating the curfew and evacuation orders. Such a pardon would allow the government to avoid addressing the petition's misconduct charges. According to Peter Irons, however, in his book *Justice Delayed*, Fred Korematsu had something to say about a pardon: "We should be the ones pardoning the government."[9] Fred Korematsu and his fellow petitioners rejected the government's offers of pardons, and Stone was forced to respond to their petition for a new trial.

Ten months after the petition had been filed, Stone finally asked Judge Patel to vacate (cancel) Fred's conviction on the basis that the government didn't think it was appropriate to defend a forty-year-old conviction. Judge Patel denied the government's request, citing that legal procedures didn't allow for the government to make such a motion after a defendant had served his sentence.[10] Without holding a full-scale hearing, she went on to vacate Fred's forty-year-old conviction on the basis that it rested on the government's presentation of "unsubstantiated facts, distortions and representations of at least one military commander, whose views were seriously infected by racism."[11]

On the heels of Judge Patel's opinion, Minoru Yasui's hearing date was set for January 16, 1984. Once again Victor Stone asked the Portland court to vacate his conviction on the same grounds that he had used in Fred Korematsu's hearing.

The judgment was bittersweet. The judge pointed out that both sides sought the same relief, so he vacated Minoru Yasui's conviction at the request of the government. At the same time he declined to consider Yasui's charges of misconduct by the government.[12]

The final case, brought by Gordon Hirabayashi in Seattle, would be heard in June 1985. Judge Donald S. Voorhees agreed that the wronged party had a right to bring his petition before the court and scheduled a full-scale hearing.

Almost a year later the *coram nobis* lawyers had their chance to prove misconduct by the government in the original trials. They went up against the Reagan Justice Department, which was determined to seek victory by bringing up the argument of sabotage, espionage, and secret coded messages.[13]

The *coram nobis* lawyers countered with the documents uncovered by Peter Irons containing information from the 1940s that two Justice Department lawyers, Edward J. Ennis and John L. Burling, had complained that Assistant Secretary of War John J. McCloy was withholding the true facts from the Supreme Court in the Korematsu, Yasui, and Hirabayashi cases. General De-Witt's reports of disloyalty and espionage had been passed off as facts. But reports by the Federal Communications Commission, Naval Intelligence, and the FBI, which refuted DeWitt's accusations, had been withheld. Further, DeWitt's report had been altered to tone down its racist diatribe.

Judge Voorhees deliberated on the evidence before him for more than seven months. Then, in his written opinion, he charged that the "government presented no evidence that the petitioner (Hirabayashi) was anything other than a law-abiding, native-born American citizen."[14] He vacated the evacuation charge, but the charge of violation of curfew remained. Gordon was quick to file an appeal.

Judge Mary M. Shroeder heard the appeal and reviewed the documents and information presented before Judge Voorhees. She concluded that the evacuation and internment had been infected with a "racial bias." She also agreed that the government had "doctored" the evidence that was originally submitted to the Supreme Court.[15] Based on these findings, Judge Shroeder ordered Judge Voorhees to vacate Gordon's curfew charge. On January 12, 1988, Judge Voorhees set aside the charges against Gordon Hirabayashi and wiped the slate clean. It had taken five years, but all three men had been vindicated. Gordon summed up the lesson: "Ancestry is not a crime."[16]

Although the CWRIC had released its recommendations in 1983, the government was slow to act. But Japanese American activists and civil rights groups continued to pressure Congress for an apology and implementation of the commission's recommendations. In 1987, Senator Spark Matsunaga of Hawaii introduced a bill that would give each surviving internee a token sum of $20,000 to amend the wrong that had been done to them and to help compensate them for their losses. Then Attorney General Edwin Meese objected to the amount of the payment and to the proposed apology. And he had support in the Senate. Senator Malcolm Wallop of Wyoming had this to say: "Honor doesn't come with a dollar sign on it, and you don't buy it back."[17] Senator Jesse Helms of North Carolina insisted that "no funds shall be appropriated under this title until the government of Japan has fairly compensated the families of men and women who were killed as a result of the ... bombing of Pearl Harbor." Helms's argument is evidence that old notions about the internment and its victims, most of whom were legal American citizens, are often difficult to change.[18] Helms couldn't see that any wrong had ever been done to the Japanese American citizenry.

In spite of Senator Helms and others, the Senate bill was finally passed in April 1988. It passed the House on the Fourth of July, sending a powerful message to the American public about the strength of the Constitution and the ability of the government to admit to an error. On August 10, 1988, President Ronald Reagan added his name to the bill, and to the national apology that it included, though he had fought such a bill initially.

Harry Kawahara had said that "[i]f you are injured, harmed, falsely imprisoned, had your character defamed, been denied your civil rights, then you seek redress. You seek restitution." Forty-six years after President Franklin Delano Roosevelt signed Executive Order 9066, the Constitution—and justice—had won out.

91

AFTERWORD

The struggle for redress and reparations had been won. For many, however, the victory came too late. Forty-six years is a long time to wait for justice, and many who had suffered the indignities of forced removal from their homes and incarceration in American-style concentration camps did not witness the righting of this injustice. They died still carrying the burden of shame that evacuation and internment had thrust upon them.

When the first payments were made—they were to be paid out in stages beginning with the oldest survivors and then proceeding to the younger ones—newspapers from coast to coast ballyhooed the $20,000 due each surviving internee. Comparatively, the newspapers gave little play to the apology and to the internment issue itself. While the sum seems large, it represented only ten cents for every dollar of actual loss. Still, sensationalized in the press and media, the payment caused resentment among many Caucasians who either did not understand or would not accept the total implications of the internment.

Yet there are precedents for monetary settlements to Americans whose constitutional rights have been violated by the government. Native Americans were awarded $800 million in 1978 for claims relating to broken treaties. And in 1980, anti–Vietnam War protesters who had been wrongfully imprisoned for a weekend were paid $10,000 each.[1] In view of the government's willingness to pay so much in these cases, it seems only reasonable that a payment of some kind was due internees who gave up so much in the wake of racial hysteria.

At a small ceremony in the Great Hall of Justice Attorney General Richard L. Thornburgh met with the eldest of the elders to distribute the first checks. He added his own apology to that of President George Bush, and what he said best explains the issue underlying redress and reparations:

> *Your struggle for redress and the events that led to today are the finest examples of what our country is about and of what we have pledged to protect and defend. Your efforts have strengthened the nation's Constitution by reaffirming the inalienability of our civil rights.*
>
> *. . . Even when that system failed you, you never lost your faith in it. On the contrary, you believed that through that system you could achieve the justice which you had been denied.*[2]

President Bush's letter of apology, which accompanied each check, echoed the attorney general's comments, though it was less eloquently stated. Admitting that "serious injustices were done to Japanese-Americans during World War II," he went on to say a "monetary sum and words alone cannot restore lost years or erase painful memories; neither can they fully convey our nation's resolve to rectify injustice and to uphold the rights of individuals."[3]

The apologies were significant, and they were directed at more than just the Japanese American community. For the first time, the United States government was acknowledging wrongdoing during this horrific period in American history and apologizing to all for abandoning the values that lie at the very heart of the nation.

Critics of redress and reparations notwithstanding, individuals joined the government in the apology. They had stood by in silence as others disregarded the principles on which this nation was founded. Yet we must wonder if history could repeat itself. Could individuals stand by in silence today? There are still calls to exclude certain citizens and resident aliens from American society. As the public was alerted to the AIDS epidemic, some self-righteous individuals and organizations urged the roundup and incarceration of victims of this tragic disease. On the heels of America's involvement in the Gulf War against Iraq, a few superpatriots endorsed the lockup of Iraqi nationals and others of Iraqi ancestry living in the United States. In southern California, squads of thugs periodically invade migrant labor camps, brandishing baseball bats and threatening the Hispanic American laborers who reside there and only wish to eke out a living.

And though they were steadfast and courageous in their efforts to win redress and reparations, Japanese Americans have not been immune to new waves of hostility. During the dismal economy of the 1980s and 1990s, Japan bashing resurfaced as flag-waving Americans smashed Japanese-made automobiles and products. The bashing didn't stop there. In Los Angeles, attacks against Japanese Americans and other Asian Americans ebbed and flowed with the strength of the American automobile industry. And then, fifty years after Executive Order 9066, as Japanese Americans were commemorating the internment with programs at the Japanese American Cultural and Community Center in 1992, threats of violence marked the event. Sadly, some pointed the finger of blame for the weak economy at

94

Japanese Americans, reproducing the same "logic" that had obscured the difference between native Japanese, on the one hand, and Japanese Americans, on the other.

The internment story has not ended. And it will not end until intolerance and racism no longer exist.

SOURCE NOTES

Three books were especially helpful to me, and I referred to them for almost all the chapters:

Daniels, Roger. *Concentration Camps: North America; Japanese in the United States and Canada during World War II.* Malabar, Fla.: Robert E. Krieger Publishing, 1981.
Personal Justice Denied. Report of the Commission on Wartime Relocation and Internment of Civilians. Washington, D.C.: U.S. Government Printing Office, 1992.
Weglyn, Michi. *Years of Infamy.* New York: Morrow Quill Paperbacks, 1976.

Chapter One

1. Walter Lord, *Day of Infamy* (New York: Holt, Rinehart and Winston, 1957), p. 12.
2. Ibid., p. 67.
3. Ibid., p. 220.
4. Frances Biddle, *In Brief Authority* (Garden City, N.Y.: Doubleday, 1962), pp. 206–7.
5. Weglyn, p. 36.
6. Roger Daniels, "Why It Happened Here," in Sue Kunitomi Embrey, *The Lost Years: 1942–46* (Los Angeles: Moonlight Publications, 1972), p. 18.

7. Weglyn, p. 67.
8. Ibid., p. 54.
9. Ibid., p. 21.

Chapter Two

1. Roger Daniels, *The Politics of Prejudice* (Berkeley: University of California Press, 1962), pp. 16–19.
2. *Personal Justice Denied*, p. 37.
3. *The Politics of Prejudice*, p. 18.
4. Ibid., pp. 2–4.
5. *Personal Justice Denied*, p. 30.
6. *The Politics of Prejudice*, p. 13.
7. *San Francisco Chronicle* and the *San Francisco Examiner*, both for May 8, 1900, as quoted in *Personal Justice Denied*, p. 32.
8. *The Politics of Prejudice*, pp. 22–23.
9. Daniel S. Davis, *Behind Barbed Wire* (New York: Dutton, 1982), p. 16.
10. *The Politics of Prejudice*, pp. 34–43. Also Davis, p. 16.
11. *Personal Justice Denied*, p. 32.
12. *The Politics of Prejudice*, pp. 61–64.
13. Ibid., pp. 85–87.
14. Ibid., p. 88.
15. *Personal Justice Denied*, p. 36.

Chapter Three

1. Franklin D. Roosevelt, Executive Order 9066, National Archives.
2. *Personal Justice Denied*, p. 85.
3. Ibid., p. 73.
4. Davis, p. 8.
5. *Personal Justice Denied*, p. 54.
6. Weglyn, pp. 45–46.
7. *Personal Justice Denied*, p. 55.
8. Davis, p. 33.
9. *Congressional Record*, December 10, 1941, p. 9630.

10. Weglyn, pp. 94–95.
11. *Personal Justice Denied*, p. 64.
12. Ibid., p. 62.
13. Ibid., p. 65.
14. Ibid., p. 82.
15. Ibid., pp. 81–82.
16. Frank J. Taylor, "The People Nobody Wants," *Saturday Evening Post*, May 9, 1942, p. 66.

Chapter Four

1. Emily Medvec, in the Introduction to Ansel Adams, *Born Free and Equal* (Washington, D.C.: Echolight Corporation, 1984), p. 8.
2. *Personal Justice Denied*, pp. 93–101.
3. Ibid., p. 102.
4. *The Lost Years*, p. 39.
5. Weglyn, pp. 54–56.
6. *Personal Justice Denied*, p. 109.
7. Davis, pp. 45–46.
8. *Personal Justice Denied*, p. 135.
9. Ibid., p. 126.
10. John Hersey, "A Mistake of Terrifically Horrible Proportions," in John Armor and Peter Wright, *Manzanar* (New York: Times Books, 1988), p. 5.
11. *Personal Justice Denied*, p. 113.
12. Peter Irons, *Justice Delayed* (Middletown, Conn.: Wesleyan University Press, 1989), p. 73.
13. Davis, p. 118.
14. Irons, p. 49.
15. Davis, p. 120.
16. *Personal Justice Denied*, p. 146.
17. Ibid., p. 147.
18. Ibid., p. 148.

Chapter Five

1. Exhibit, "A More Perfect Union: Japanese Americans and the U.S. Constitution," at the National Museum

of American History, Smithsonian Institution, Washington, D.C.
2. Weglyn, p. 217.
3. Monica Itoi Sone, *Nisei Daughter* (Boston: Atlantic Monthly Press, 1953), p. 192.
4. Vincent Tajiri, *Through Innocent Eyes* (Los Angeles: Keiro Services Press, 1990), p. 25.
5. Ibid., p. 38.
6. Violet Kazue deCristoforo, *A Victim of the Japanese Evacuation and Resettlement Study (JERS)*. An affidavit (Monterey, Calif.: V. K. deCristoforo, 1987), p. 11.
7. John Armor and Peter Wright, *Manzanar* (New York: Times Books, 1988), p. 95.
8. *Concentration Camps*, p. 99.
9. Davis, pp. 100–01.
10. deCristoforo, pp. 11–12.
11. *Personal Justice Denied*, pp. 193–94.

Chapter Six
1. Captain George Aki, quoted in Chester Tanaka, *Go for Broke: A Pictorial History of the Japanese American 100th Infantry Battalion and 442d Regimental Combat Team* (Richmond, Calif.: Go For Broke, 1982), p. iii.
2. *Personal Justice Denied*, p. 253.
3. Ibid., p. 254.
4. Ibid.
5. Ibid., p. 256.
6. Tanaka, p. 4.
7. Ibid., p. 11.
8. Ibid., p. 13.
9. Ibid.
10. Exhibit, "A More Perfect Union," at the National Museum of History, Smithsonian Institution, Washington, D.C.
11. *Personal Justice Denied*, p. 256.

12. Tanaka, p. 50.
13. *Personal Justice Denied*, p. 257.
14. Tanaka, p. 51.
15. Ibid., pp. 90–99.
16. Ibid., p. 103.
17. *Personal Justice Denied*, p. 258.
18. Ibid. Also Tanaka, p. 123.
19. Tanaka, p. 1.
20. "Stilwell Pays Tribute to Nisei Killed in Italy," *Los Angeles Times*, December 9, 1945.
21. *Personal Justice Denied*, p. 260.

Chapter Seven

1. *Personal Justice Denied*, p. 215.
2. Ibid., p. 216.
3. Ibid.
4. Ibid., p. 221.
5. Ibid.
6. Ibid., p. 227.
7. Davis, p. 122.
8. *Personal Justice Denied*, pp. 232–33.
9. Ibid., p. 252.

Chapter Eight

1. *Personal Justice Denied*, p. 118.
2. *The Lost Years*, front matter.
3. *Federal Register*, Vol. 41, No. 35, February 20, 1976.
4. Irons, p. 4.
5. Ibid., p. 49.
6. Ibid., p. 73.
7. Ibid., p. 76.
8. Ibid., p. 6.
9. Ibid., p. 21.
10. Ibid., p. 23.
11. Dale Minami, "Coram Nobis and Redress," in Sue Kunitomi Embrey, ed., *50 Year Remembrance: Japanese American Internment* (Los Angeles: Japanese

American Cultural and Community Center, 1992),
   pp. 13–14.
12. Irons, p. 29.
13. Ibid., pp. 30–41.
14. Ibid., p. 42.
15. Ibid., p. 45.
16. Ibid., p. 46.
17. Quoted in *Time*, May 2, 1988, p. 70.
18. Hersey, pp. 64–66.

Afterword

1. Armor, p. 155.
2. Quoted in *US News and World Report*, October 22, 1990, p. 19.
3. Quoted in *Los Angeles Times*, October 10, 1990.

GLOSSARY

alien: a person born in a country other than the one in which he or she lives

assembly center: a "temporary" facility used to house those who were forced to move away from the West Coast of the United States

evacuee: the government term for a person of Japanese ancestry who was forced to leave the West Coast of the United States

fifth column: a secret, subversive army of residents who act in sympathy with the enemy

infamy: strong condemnation as a result of a shameful act

internee: evacuee; a person who was forced to inhabit the government's "pioneer" communities

interventionist: a person who favors involvement in the affairs of another country

isolationist: a person who favors noninvolvement in the affairs of another country

Issei: immigrants from Japan

Nisei: children of the Issei born in the United States

redress: the setting right of a wrong

relocation center: the government term for a permanent wartime camp; a concentration camp

reparations: compensation for a wrong or an injury

102

Sansei: children of the Nisei, grandchildren of the Issei, born in the United States

Shikata ga nai: it cannot be helped; it must be done

yellow peril: a fear based on racism that Asians, or yellow-skinned people, would conquer and make subjects of Caucasians

SELECTED
BIBLIOGRAPHY

Adams, Ansel. Edited by Emily Medvec. *Born Free and Equal.* Washington, D.C.: Echolight Corporation, 1984.

Armor, John, and Peter Wright. *Manzanar.* New York: Times Books, 1988.

Biddle, Frances. *In Brief Authority.* Garden City, N.Y.: Doubleday, 1962.

Conrat, Maisie, and Richard Conrat. *Executive Order 9066: The Internment of 110,000 Japanese Americans.* Cambridge, Mass.: MIT Press, 1972.

Cross, Jennifer. *Justice Denied.* New York: Scholastic Book Services, 1972.

Daniels, Roger. *Concentration Camps: North America; Japanese in the United States and Canada during World War II.* Malabar, Fla.: Robert E. Krieger Publishing, 1981.

Daniels, Roger. *The Politics of Prejudice.* Berkeley: University of California Press, 1962.

Davis, Daniel S. *Behind Barbed Wire.* New York: Dutton, 1982.

deCristoforo, Violet Kazue. *A Victim of the Japanese Evacuation and Resettlement Study (JERS).* An affidavit. Monterey, Calif.: V. K. deCristoforo, 1987.

Embrey, Sue Kunitomi. *The Lost Years: 1942–46.* Los Angeles: Moonlight Publications, 1972.

Embrey, Sue Kunitomi, et al. *50 Year Remembrance: Japanese American Internment.* Los Angeles: Japanese American Cultural and Community Center, 1992.

Gesensway, Deborah, and Mindy Roseman. *Beyond Words.* Ithaca, N.Y.: Cornell University Press, 1987.

Houston, Jeanne Wakatsuki, and James D. Houston. *Farewell to Manzanar.* New York: Bantam Books, 1973.

Irons, Peter. *Justice Delayed.* Middletown, Conn.: Wesleyan University Press, 1989.

Kitano, Harry. *The Japanese Americans.* New York: Chelsea House, 1987.

Leathers, Noel L. *The Japanese in America.* Minneapolis, Minn.: Lerner Publications, 1967.

Lehman, Anthony L. *Birthright of Barbed Wire.* Los Angeles: Westernlore Press, 1970.

Lord, Walter. *Day of Infamy.* New York: Holt, Rinehart and Winston, 1957.

Merritt, Ralph P. "Pete," Jr. *Death Valley—Its Impounded Americans.* Death Valley, Calif.: Death Valley '49ers, 1987.

Okazaki, Steven, et al. *Unfinished Business: The Japanese American Internment Cases.* A PBS-TV film. Mouchette Films.

Okubo, Mine. *Citizen 13660.* Seattle, Wash.: University of Washington Press, 1991.

Personal Justice Denied. Report of the Commission on Wartime Relocation and Internment of Civilians. Washington, D.C.: U.S. Government Printing Office, 1992.

Prange, Gordon W. *At Dawn We Slept.* New York: McGraw-Hill, 1981.

Sone, Monica Itoi. *Nisei Daughter.* Boston: Atlantic Monthly Press, 1953.

Stillwell, Paul. *Air Raid: Pearl Harbor!* Annapolis, Md.: Naval Institute Press, 1981.

Stuart, C. C. *Inside View Japanese American Evacuee Center 1941–1945.* McGehee, Ark.: McGehee Publishing, 1979.

Tajiri, Vincent. *Through Innocent Eyes.* Los Angeles: Keiro Services Press, 1990.

Tanaka, Chester. *Go For Broke: A Pictorial History of the Japanese American 100th Infantry Battalion and 442d Regimental Combat Team.* Richmond, Calif.: Go For Broke, 1982.

Tateishi, John. *And Justice for All.* New York: Random House, 1984.

Weglyn, Michi. *Years of Infamy.* New York: Morrow Quill Paperbacks, 1976.

Yatsushiro, Toshio. *Politics and Cultural Values: The World War II Japanese Relocation Centers and the United States.* New York: Arno Press, 1978.

INDEX

and Internment of
Civilians, the (CWRIC),
23, 81, 85, 88, 90
Roosevelt, Franklin D.,
12, 21, 22, 23, 24, 31,
32, 35, 48, 58, 67, 71,
72, 91

Sansei, 79, 81, 82, 83, 85
Santa Anita Assembly
Center, 28, 41, 42, 43,
44
Seki, Sumiko Seo, 41, 44
Short, General Walter C.,
23, 28
Social Security Act of
1972, 84
Sone, Monica, 50
Stillwell, Major General
Joseph W., 29, 67, 68
Stimson, Henry L., 29, 33,
70
Student leave program,
56, 57, 58
Sumida, Marshall, 43

Taketa, George, 56
Tamai, Joyce, 74, 77, 78,
79
Tanforan Assembly
Center, 41
Tokushige, Shizuko, 43, 48
Truman, Harry S., 67, 79
Tsuneishi, Sally, 45, 52, 76
Tule Lake Relocation
Center, 40, 49, 55, 60

United States
Constitution, 13, 14, 19,
20, 29, 41, 72, 85, 87,
91, 93
United States Congress,
12, 13, 18, 25, 30, 31,
71, 84, 85
United States Supreme
Court, 39, 40, 58, 72,
85, 86, 87, 88, 90
Usui, Mitsuo, 27, 60, 61,
68, 72, 73, 77

Voluntary evacuation, 34,
35

War Relocation Authority
(WRA), 36, 40, 44, 50,
52, 56, 58, 72, 74
Wartime Civil Control
Administration, 36, 43,
44
Washington, 12, 20, 28,
29, 31, 33, 86
Watanabe, Teru, 40
Western Defense
Command, 28, 38, 57,
64, 70, 71

Yamaga, Henry, 25
Yamamoto, Joe, 38
Yamashita, Kanshi, 51
Yamashita, Stan, 36
Yasui, Minoru, 39, 40, 86,
87, 88, 89, 90

ABOUT THE AUTHOR

Larry Dane Brimner's first book for Watts, *BMX Freestyle*, was an International Reading Association Children's Choice Book for 1988, and his *Animals That Hibernate* (Watts) was named to the "Best Children's Science Book" list of 1991.

During his early childhood on Alaska's remote Kodiak Island, reading and making up stories was a part of his daily family life, and Larry traces his love of books to that time. He began writing for publication during his twenty-year career as a teacher. Now a full-time writer, he has published more than two hundred stories and articles and many award-winning books.

Larry Dane Brimner is a member of the Authors Guild and the Society of Children's Book Writers and Illustrators. He lives in Southern California and the Rocky Mountains.